Sarah Dueweke

Primal Kitchen

real food recipes

Photography
Elizabeth Clarkson

PENGUIN BOOKS

PENGUIN

UK | USA | Canada | Ireland | Australia
India | New Zealand | South Africa | China

Penguin is an imprint of the Penguin Random House group of companies, whose addresses can be found at global.penguinrandomhouse.com.

Penguin
Random House
New Zealand

First published by Penguin Random House New Zealand, 2015

10 9 8 7 6 5 4 3 2 1

Design by Sarah Healey © Penguin Random House New Zealand
Typeset in Scala by Sarah Healey
Photography on pages 5 and 7 taken at Ponsonby Central, Auckland
Colour separation by Image Centre Ltd
Printed and bound in China by South China Printing Company

A catalogue record for this book is available from the National Library of New Zealand.

ISBN 978-0-14-357244-2

penguinrandomhouse.co.nz

CONTENTS

MY STORY

I can't remember a time when the word 'diet' was not in my vocabulary. My life's history of weight maintenance began at a very young age. The middle daughter of three girls, I was a short, chubby-ish brunette in between two slender, blonde sisters (seriously, whose joke was that?!).

I could list a million and one euphemisms for 'fat' that I was given while growing up, all meaning the same thing. I have vivid memories of trying on school clothes in a girls' dressing room and being told I was a bit too 'thick' or 'heavy' for certain outfits. I began each day with a bowl of cereal for breakfast – something labelled 'Heart Healthy' by the American Heart Association (yet somehow still loaded with sugar . . .). My mother always tried to pack healthy lunches for me, usually a sandwich, a fat-free granola bar and a box of juice. Dinner was your typical meat–veg–carbs, maybe some chicken and veggie pasta or something similar. By most people's standards, I ate pretty healthily for the typical American kid! We never had chips or sugary soda drinks or junk food. But I was somehow still a bit overweight throughout my whole childhood. I tried dozens of diets, always the low-fat or fat-free options, but nothing seemed to work. I was convinced that my body was just 'one of those' and I could never be skinny. Skinny: it's funny how that was always my goal. Not healthy. Just *skinny*.

I reached my peak weight at the age of 21 and sincerely believed that I was doomed. How I longed to be able to wear a bikini at the beach like all the other beautiful, *skinny* girls!

The summer after I turned 21, everything was crazy. I was working full-time as an intern, and taking summer courses, and doing another part-time job on the weekends. One morning, a few weeks into this insane schedule, I stepped on the bathroom scales and, much to my surprise, I had lost three pounds! (That's a kilo and a half.) My working non-stop all week long had caused me to forget to eat a few meals. Suddenly, I was super-motivated to keep that weight-loss train in motion. I began a calorie diary, writing down every single thing I ate and tallying it up at the end of the day. At the start, I was eating about 1000 calories (or 4000 kJ) a day. I knew that if I wanted to lose more weight, I would have to start exercising so that I could burn more calories than I was eating. Calories in, calories out – right?

Summer ended and regular classes started up again. I had a schedule that was less hectic, but I was more motivated than ever to keep losing weight. I started going to the university's gym every day, and after a few months had my daily calorie intake down to about 500. I could get down to 450 if I really tried. I lost even more weight. I also started losing my hair. I couldn't sleep at night and I would feel dizzy getting out of bed in the mornings. It seems incredibly obvious in hindsight that I had developed a problem, but I couldn't see it. All I could see were the numbers on the scales. I even loved hearing people tell me I was looking *too* skinny.

I spent the year after university in an obsessive state, looking at every single item of food that came near me like it was a

number. Like it was just calories. However, despite my food demons constantly lurking around me, I never lost my love of cooking. I was really good at feeding other people . . . just not myself. I loved cooking so much that I followed a childhood dream of mine and enrolled at culinary school in 2009. I scoffed at everyone who told me, 'There's no such thing as a skinny chef!'

I began working at a local gym to help pay for school and, while my food obsession was still there, I began to take on more of an interest in fitness. I was surrounded by beautiful, strong women and I wanted to get strong, too!

In 2010, a friend of mine told me about this crazy gym he had joined called CrossFit. 'It's awesome, and we're doing this paleo challenge thing . . . ,' he said. Uh, what? Pale-who? He gave me the lowdown on paleo and bet me that I couldn't do it. 'Oh yeah? I'll show you!' I went home and did some research on paleo – and immediately became obsessed. Fat is good for me? Grains are bad?! I devoured every article I could find on paleo/primal research, and it all just made sense. I decided primal was the way to go, which allowed me to eat dairy products in moderation.

It was scary at first, suddenly eating butter and bacon and things I never thought I could have, but after a bit of hesitation I gradually accepted the fact that eating fat wasn't going to kill me. I soon ditched my fat-free, low-cal yoghurts and fat-free toast with margarine (good god, I was consuming a *lot* of chemicals!). I dove into omelettes with avocado and steak salads with fatty feta cheese. I was getting healthier, and I was feeling better all the time. My hair was getting thick again. I was growing muscle. And I was sleeping like a baby.

A year later, I joined my first CrossFit gym in Chantilly, Virginia. It was like finding a whole club full of people who lived and ate paleo! I started lifting heavy weights, and eating – a lot. I had never felt better. I was even getting pretty good at the fitness stuff!

On 1 November 2011 I fulfilled another long-time dream of mine and moved to New Zealand. One of the first places I went when I settled in was CrossFit Central Wellington. There, I met a whole new family of fitness freaks and paleo nerds who shared my love of healthy living (and eating!). Here in Wellington, I also met my good friend Vinnie, whom I introduced to the primal lifestyle. After finding great success with his new-found love of healthy living, we started our own primal foods company – Primal Kitchen – where we make and deliver delicious, healthy primal meals and snacks. (Check us out at www.primalkitchen.co.nz.) Now I have developed my own personal collection of paleo/primal recipes that I've cooked for myself and friends over and over again, and I am happy to share them with you. Food should never be a scary thing when you're looking for great health. Food is your ally! Your body needs it. These are my favourite recipes for clean, healthy eating – I hope you enjoy them, too.

ORGANIC

WHAT IS PRIMAL ABOUT?

If you are new to the primal lifestyle, you might be asking: 'What does eating primal even mean?' The simple answer that is often given is to 'eat like a caveman', but that's a poor generalisation. We're not all out there eating bugs and hunting woolly mammoths. The idea of 'eating like a caveman' is more of a guideline to teach us to eat the foods that our bodies are made to consume.

Living primal means eating the way humans had adapted to do for the 200,000 years before the development of modern agriculture. That means a diet high in protein and fat, in addition to healthy carbohydrates. The primal lifestyle is very similar to the paleo one. They both encourage a diet of mostly grass-fed meats, seafood and eggs, in addition to nutritious vegetables, fruits, nuts and seeds. No grains, legumes, soy or refined sugars allowed. Packaged products and lab-created 'foods'? Forget about it. There are varying opinions on what is allowed on a strictly paleo diet versus what is allowed when eating the slightly less restrictive primal diet. The main differences are that paleo eating excludes all dairy products, including milk, cheese, yoghurt and butter (ingredients that are allowed in limited quantities on a primal diet), and alcohol (primal eaters are allowed wine or occasional other alcoholic beverages). Paleo eaters also limit their intake of the starchier fruits and vegetables, such as kumara, apples and bananas, whereas people living primal do not restrict their carbohydrate intake quite as much.

For a lot of people, the idea of such a drastic change in diet is pretty scary. Primal eating may go against a lot of what you thought to be true about healthy eating. We're all used to being told to stay away from fatty foods, when in fact our bodies run on fat. It is our primary source of energy! If you're going to live primal, you have to understand that eating fat will not necessarily make you fat. It is the *source* of the fats we consume that is important to monitor; we must be sure to include plenty of natural fats in our diets, including animal fats and natural oils.

Scientific backing for the primal diet is very compelling, and the primal lifestyle is gaining increasing popularity with medical professionals around the world. It is believed that modern diseases and chronic health issues such as obesity, cancer, multiple sclerosis and diabetes have only become major problems in our society since the human diet changed from primarily meats and vegetables to meals consisting predominantly of grains, refined sugars and, more recently, processed foods. As people have begun to recognise this, some have started to try eating a bit differently; perhaps a gluten-free diet. From a primal point of view this is a step in the right direction, although many (if not most) gluten-free foods on the market still contain grains and a shocking amount of sugar. Eating primal is the next big step. Removing unnecessary grains (such as whole wheat, corn and rice), legumes (including lentils, beans and soy products) and refined sugars from your diet, and replacing them with nutritious fat and protein for energy and ideal health, will have you feeling better than you ever thought possible.

So, what does the typical day of a primal eater look like? I usually start my day with two hard-boiled eggs and half an avocado for breakfast, or a small dish of homemade granola (pages

16 and 19) with Greek yoghurt. For lunch I'll have my Kitchen Sink Salad (page 57) – loaded with all the seasonal vegetables I get from my local veggie markets and some leftover chicken or other meat to make sure I get my fat and protein. If I'm hungry in the afternoon before a workout, I'll grab one or two Energy Bites (page 20) from my freezer, or have a piece of fresh fruit like an apple or a banana. Dinner usually consists of roasted vegetables and a slow-cooked meat dish from my handy slow-cooker; and if it feels like a night for something sweet for dessert, I might just have some Sweet Kumara Ice Cream (page 127) stashed in the freezer! A big point about going paleo or primal is to forget about what you think meals are 'supposed' to be. I've been known to eat a leftover lamb steak for breakfast – cold, in fact straight out of the refrigerator. It doesn't sound like a typical breakfast food, but the point is – *it's food.* Good food! And I never experience the mid-morning sugar crash that most people get after eating bread and/or cereal for breakfast – no sugar = no sugar crash.

Of course, each person will eat different proportions in terms of protein–fats–carbs, depending on their personal needs. This will also depend on whether they are looking simply to maintain a healthy diet or specifically want to lose weight. Those who are very active are likely to eat more of the starchier vegetables and fruits to fill themselves up, than will sedentary people. Paleo and primal eating emphasises eating until you are full. If you are eating the right foods, your body will tell you when enough is enough. You are less likely to overeat broccoli and roast chicken than bread or pasta!

In addition to a healthy diet, people living a primal lifestyle typically focus on regular exercise, healthy sleeping habits and getting plenty of sunshine and play time to avoid stress. This is meant to mirror the lifestyles that our hunter-gatherer ancestors lived – the way our bodies are made to work, not only to survive but to thrive!

For more information on the paleo/primal diet, and the scientific research behind it, be sure to check these out:

- *Why We Get Fat: And What To Do About It*, by Gary Taubes (published by Anchor Books/Random House, 2011)

- *The Paleo Solution: The Original Human Diet*, by Robb Wolf (published by Victory Belt Publishing, 2010)

- *The Primal Blueprint*, by Mark Sisson (published by Primal Nutrition, Inc., 2009; updated 2013).

PRIMAL PANTRY ESSENTIALS

Eating primal does not mean you need obscure and expensive ingredients – in fact, the ingredients in this book can be found in most grocery stores. For a lot of people just starting out with primal eating, the big scary question is: 'Okay, so what *can* I eat?' These guidelines will give you an idea of the best way to stock your own Primal Kitchen for everyday healthy cooking.

Meat, fish and eggs

In a primal or paleo diet, meat, fish and eggs are essential. In the past you've probably been told to steer clear of the fattier cuts of meat, egg yolks, the skin on your chicken . . . basically all the most delicious parts! It's unfortunate that the terrible myth that all fat is bad for you has been taught for so long, but the good news is that when you're eating primal, all of that tasty stuff is fair game. It's always best to opt for grass-fed and free-farmed meats, free-range chicken and eggs, and wild-caught fish whenever possible. The saying 'we are what we eat' may be a cliché, but it's the truth. We also are what we eat eats! A chicken that's left free to forage for bugs and grass is a happier, healthier chicken than one stuffed in a cage getting fed a diet of corn and grains. It's also much more delicious.

Fruit and veg

Most fruits and vegetables can be part of a balanced primal diet. They are full of the fibre and vitamins necessary for a healthy body and serve as the carbohydrates in a primal diet. Fresh produce is always best whenever possible. Pre-packaged fruits and vegetables are often processed with other ingredients, for example dried fruits with added sugar or frozen vegetables in pre-cooked sauces. These are *not* primal. It's important to always read the labels of any packaged products to make sure you know what is really in them. You'll be surprised to learn how many foods contain added sugar!

Dairy

Dairy is one of the main elements separating the paleo from the primal diet. For those on a strict paleo diet, dairy products are not allowed. However, primal eaters may have some full-fat dairy products. I find the dairy-or-not dilemma to be simply a matter of personal preference. Some people have difficulty digesting milk and cheese, while others (myself included) have no problems at all with dairy. This book contains some recipes with milk or cheese, but usually includes dairy-free options as well. Coconut milk and unsweetened almond milk are great alternatives to dairy products in cooking. If you are eating dairy, it's important to remember to always opt for the full-fat options. Any dairy product that is 'low-fat' did not get that way naturally.

Cooking fats

I can't stress the importance of fat in primal eating strongly enough! Fat is essential for energy, and it's pretty damn tasty, too – but it must come from the right sources. Natural oils like coconut oil, olive oil, avocado oil and tree nut oils, in addition to natural animal fats like bacon fat, lard, duck fat or butter, are all great fats to cook with. These are *natural* oils and fats that undergo minimal processing before they make it to your kitchen. It is imperative to avoid the mad-scientist, lab-created hydrogenated oils found in most packaged foods. These weird chemical concoctions were not made to be healthy – they were made because they were cheaper! Vegetable oil, soybean oil, seeds oils and canola oil are all examples of hydrogenated oils created in a lab in order to have a long shelf-life. They are definitely not something you want in your food.

Nuts and seeds

Tree nuts and seeds are fantastic sources of fat and protein. These include by-products of nuts and seeds, such as nut flours, butters and milks. Almond flour in particular is found in a lot of primal cooking and baking. It's important to remember, though, that nuts and seeds are very nutrient-dense and should be eaten in moderation.

Sweeteners

Cooking primal allows for the occasional use of natural sweeteners. These include honey, blackstrap molasses, pure maple syrup, date paste (or other natural fruit sweeteners) and one of the newest ingredients on the market – coconut sugar (although this is easy to abuse!). In addition, primal eaters can have dark chocolate, but should opt for a higher cocoa content whenever possible (at least 70% cocoa solids). Real dark chocolate should only have four ingredients: cocoa mass, cocoa butter, natural vanilla and sugar. Compound chocolate, which can be found everywhere on grocery store shelves, is in my opinion an abomination. It's a blend of cocoa, sugar and vegetable oils that masquerades as chocolate, and it's definitely not primal! No matter what natural sweeteners you may choose to use, they should all be considered once-in-a-while treats and not part of your everyday diet.

Supplements

Dietary supplements are not required on a primal diet, although they are not forbidden, either. When you're eating all-primal foods, you should already be getting a healthy balance of everything your body needs! Some choose to include whey protein powder or 'superfood' boosts (like spirulina or wheatgrass), which are fine as long as they do not contain added sugars or preservatives. These items can be found in health food stores and some pharmacies.

Flours and baking ingredients

Primal baking uses an array of different flours in place of grain-based flours, which are not part of a primal diet. Once difficult to find, these are now available in most grocery stores as gluten-free baking has become more popular. The flours used most often are:

- **Almond flour** – also referred to as ground almonds, almond flour makes cake moist and dense. Any recipe calling for almond flour can be replaced with another nut flour (such as hazelnut flour).

- **Coconut flour** – dried, finely ground coconut. This makes a great primal baking ingredient, especially if you are cooking for friends with nut allergies. Note that coconut flour is incredibly absorbent. You will typically need more liquid (or less flour) when baking with it.

- **Tapioca flour** – another nut-free primal flour, made from cassava root. Tapioca flour makes primal baking very light and fluffy. Used on its own, however, it can give a rather spongy texture to baked goods. It works well in combination with almond flour or coconut flour.

- **Arrowroot flour** – very similar to tapioca flour, just made from arrowroot. It can be used interchangeably with tapioca flour.

- **Ground linseed** – also referred to as flax meal, ground linseed is another rather dense primal baking ingredient. It has a rich flavour and a little goes a long way!

PROTEINS	Allowed	Eat in moderation	Just say no
Meat, fish and eggs	Beef, lamb, poultry, pork, goat, venison and other game meat (including offal cuts); free-range, grass-fed and hormone-free meat is always preferred Fish and shellfish Eggs	Naturally cured meats, like honey-cured bacon	Meats processed with sugar and chemical preservatives, like certain sausages, jerky and bacon Canned meats or fish marinated in sugar, processed oils and preservatives

FATS	Allowed	Eat in moderation	Just say no
Cooking fats	Fruit oils, such as avocado oil, olive oil and coconut oil Butter and natural animal fats (duck fat, bacon fat, lard) Tree nut oils, such as hazelnut oil, walnut oil and macadamia oil		Highly processed oils, such as canola, vegetable oil, soybean oil and peanut oil Shortening/Kremelta Artificial spreads/ margarine
Dairy		Full-fat dairy products, including milk, cheese, yoghurt, sour cream, crème fraîche and kefir (fermented milk and yoghurt)	Low-fat, fat-free or artificial 'dairy' products
Nuts and seeds		Tree nuts such as almonds, brazil nuts, cashews, hazelnuts, macadamias, pecans, pine nuts, pistachios and walnuts Seeds such as chia, pumpkin, sesame and sunflower seeds	

SWEET STUFF	Allowed	Once in a while	Just say no
		Date paste, dark chocolate (at least 70% cocoa solids), coconut sugar, honey, pure maple syrup and black strap molasses	Refined sugars such as caster sugar, icing sugar, golden syrup and corn syrup, and any artificial sweeteners (these are chemical monstrosities)

CARBOHYDRATES	Allowed	Eat in moderation	Just say no
Fruits	Fresh or frozen berries, including blackberries, blueberries, boysenberries, cranberries, raspberries and strawberries	Fresh apples, apricots, bananas, cherries, coconut, dates, feijoas, figs, goji berries, gooseberries, grapefruit, grapes, kiwifruit, lemons, limes, lychees, mandarins, mangos, melons, nectarines, oranges, papayas, passionfruit, peaches, pears, pineapple, plums, pomegranates, quince, raspberries, strawberries and tamarind Dried fruits or fruit juices that contain no added sugars or preservatives	Dried fruits, fruit juices or canned fruits that contain added sugars, syrups or preservatives
Vegetables	Lower-starch vegetables such as asparagus, capsicum, bok choy, broccoli, cabbage, cauliflower, celery, chillies, courgettes, cucumbers, daikon, eggplant, fennel, fiddlehead ferns, kale, kohlrabi, leeks, lettuce, mushrooms, onions, puha, radicchio, radish, rhubarb, salad greens (rocket, mesclun, baby spinach, etc.), seaweed, silverbeet, spinach, squash, Swiss chard, turnips, watercress and witloof	Starchier but nutritious vegetables like artichokes, beetroot, Brussels sprouts, carrots, celeriac, Jerusalem artichokes, kumara, okra, parsnips, peas, pumpkin, swedes, taro root and tomatoes	High-starch, low-nutrient vegetables like white potatoes and sweetcorn (which is actually a grain masquerading as a vegetable)
Legumes			Soy beans and products, chickpeas, lentils, beans, etc.
Grains			Wheat, oats, rice, barley, etc. Sweetcorn

Fuel Up

Power-packed breakfasts
to energise your day

This is the recipe that started it all. I'd been doing primal cooking and baking for quite a while, but when I made this for my friends at CrossFit Central Wellington it was an instant hit. My friends' support (and constant heckling for recipes, especially this one!) are really what moved me to write this book. Just beware . . . it's pretty addictive.

FAMOUS CINNAMON VANILLA GRANOLA

Makes approximately 14 servings (½ cup each)

- 2½ cups chopped raw almonds
- 1 cup chopped raw cashews
- ¾ cup raw sunflower seeds
- ½ cup raw pumpkin seeds
- 1½ cups coconut threads
- ½ cup almond flour
- 2½ tsp ground cinnamon
- 1¼ tsp sea salt
- ¼ cup liquid honey
- ⅓ cup melted coconut oil
- 1½ tsp Vanilla Extract (page 168)
- 1 cup sultanas
- ¾ cup chopped dates

Preheat oven to 150°C. Line a large roasting pan with non-stick baking paper.

Combine almonds, cashews, sunflower seeds, pumpkin seeds, coconut, almond flour, cinnamon, sea salt, honey, melted coconut oil and vanilla, and stir well.

Spread granola mixture over the lined roasting pan and place in oven.

Bake for a total of approximately 1 hour, stirring every 15 minutes to ensure the nuts do not burn. Stir in the sultanas and dates halfway through baking.

Allow to cool completely in the pan, then store in an airtight container at room temperature.

Serve with Greek yoghurt, or coconut milk for a dairy-free breakfast.

This is the other variation of breakfast granola I developed for my hungry CrossFit friends. It's really just a reason to eat chocolate for breakfast! Serve it up with some thick Greek yoghurt and sliced banana.

COCOA HAZELNUT GRANOLA

Makes approximately 16 servings (½ cup each)

- 3½ cups chopped almonds
- 1½ cups chopped hazelnuts
- 1 cup sunflower seeds
- 2 cups coconut threads
- ½ cup almond flour
- 3 tbsp Dutch-processed cocoa powder
- 1 tsp ground cinnamon
- 1¼ tsp sea salt
- ¼ cup liquid honey
- ⅓ cup melted coconut oil
- 1½ tsp Vanilla Extract (page 168)
- 1 cup sultanas
- ¾ cup chopped dates

Preheat oven to 150°C. Line a large roasting pan with non-stick baking paper.

Combine almonds, hazelnuts, sunflower seeds, coconut, almond flour, cocoa powder, cinnamon, sea salt, honey, melted coconut oil and vanilla, and stir well.

Spread granola mixture over the lined roasting pan and place in oven.

Bake for a total of approximately 1 hour, stirring every 15 minutes to ensure the nuts do not burn. Add the sultanas and dates halfway through baking.

Allow to cool completely in the pan, then store in an airtight container at room temperature.

These little flavour bombs are the perfect breakfast or snack on the go, when you have no time to mess around with cooking. You can make a big batch of these guys and store them in the freezer for any time you need a fast and filling treat.

ENERGY BITES

Makes 20

- 24 pitted dates
- 1 tsp Vanilla Extract (page 168)
- 1½ tbsp instant coffee powder
- 3 tbsp Dutch-processed cocoa powder
- ¾ cup walnuts
- ¾ cup hazelnuts
- 1 tbsp melted coconut oil
- ½ cup coconut threads

Place dates in a bowl, cover with boiling water and allow to soak for 10 minutes.

Drain dates and place in the bowl of a food processor with the vanilla, coffee and cocoa. Blend until the mixture starts to come together.

Add walnuts and hazelnuts to the food processor and process until they are chopped fairly small and the mixture starts to form a sticky ball. Drizzle in the coconut oil last, and continue to mix until fully incorporated.

Scoop out the mixture in amounts of about 1½ tablespoons at a time and roll into bite-sized balls. Spread coconut over a large plate, then roll the balls in it to coat them.

Store in an airtight container in the refrigerator or freezer.

Cook's Note

You can use any combination of your favourite nuts or dried fruit to make these (just be sure to use dried fruit with no added sugar!). You could also add ½ cup of your favourite protein powder or 2 teaspoons of spirulina to the mix, for an extra boost!

This recipe is for my dad, the spirulina king. He puts a sprinkle of spirulina on his breakfast every day, and he's been doing it since before it was cool. He's also one of the healthiest guys I know! The mighty green spirulina powder is a kind of blue-green algae, good for the health of your immune system. It'll turn your smoothie a gorgeous shade of green (although it is an optional add-in if algae isn't your thing). The ripe banana and frozen raspberries add just the right amount of sweetness to this smoothie, while the healthy fat from the avocado and the coconut milk will keep you feeling full all morning.

SUPER-POWERED BREAKFAST SMOOTHIE

Serves 1

½ ripe banana
¼ cup frozen raspberries
¼ large avocado (or ½ a small one)
¾ cup coconut milk
½ tsp spirulina powder (optional)
1 scoop whey protein (optional)

Put all the ingredients in a blender and mix until smooth.

Pour into a glass or portable drink container and enjoy your super-powered breakfast!

Cook's Note

Using frozen raspberries right out of the freezer will make your smoothie extra thick.

Whey protein and spirulina can be found in most grocery stores or in health supplement stores.

A lot of my primal baking uses equal parts of coconut flour and almond flour. I've found that using just almond flour makes food too heavy, and often using only coconut flour will make it too dry. The combination of the two in this recipe is just right! These pancakes are also a great way to use up those last few bananas of the bunch that got just a little too ripe.

CINNAMON BANANA PANCAKES

Serves 4 (2 pancakes each)

¼ cup almond flour
¼ cup coconut flour
½ tsp baking soda
½ tsp baking powder
1 tbsp ground cinnamon
¼ tsp salt
2 over-ripe bananas
4 eggs, whisked
butter or coconut oil as needed
liquid honey or pure maple syrup to serve
extra sliced banana to serve (optional)
extra ground cinnamon to serve (optional)
Greek yoghurt to serve (optional)

Mix almond flour, coconut flour, baking soda, baking powder, cinnamon and salt together.

Mash bananas until they're nice and smooth, then whisk them together with the eggs.

Stir the banana mixture into the dry ingredients and whisk until thoroughly combined.

Heat a non-stick pancake pan over a medium-high heat. Add a few teaspoons of butter or coconut oil to the pan to melt and allow it to spread around over the surface.

Pour about ¼ cup of batter per pancake into the pan and cook for a few minutes, keeping watch. Once bubbles start to form around the edge of the pancake, flip it and cook the other side for another minute. Continue until all the batter is used, adding more butter or oil to the pan as needed. Place cooked pancakes in a stack on a warmed plate and cover with a clean tea towel.

Serve warm with a drizzle of honey or pure maple syrup and sliced banana, cinnamon and a dollop of Greek yoghurt, if using.

Making pancakes for a Sunday morning treat is something I love to do, and using sweet, fresh fruits like oranges and blueberries together makes them extra special. I like to serve these up with a smear of butter and a drizzle of honey – and of course lots of extra berries on the side!

BLUEBERRY ORANGE PANCAKES

Serves 4 (2 pancakes each)

½ cup almond flour
¼ cup coconut flour
½ tsp baking soda
½ tsp baking powder
¼ tsp salt
¼ cup melted coconut oil or butter
¼ cup full-fat milk or coconut milk
2 tbsp liquid honey
5 eggs, whisked
zest and juice of 1 orange
½ cup blueberries
butter or coconut oil as needed
butter to serve (optional)

Stir almond flour, coconut flour, baking soda, baking powder and salt together.

In a separate bowl, whisk coconut oil or melted butter, milk or coconut milk, honey, eggs, orange juice and orange zest together.

Whisk the egg mixture together with the flour mixture, then stir in the blueberries.

Heat a non-stick pancake pan over a medium-high heat. Add a few teaspoons of butter or coconut oil to the pan to melt and allow it to spread around over the surface.

Pour about ¼ cup of batter per pancake into the pan. Cook for a few minutes, until the edges start to brown, then flip and cook the other side for another minute until golden. Continue until all the batter is used, adding more butter or oil to the pan as needed. To keep the pancakes hot until ready to serve, place them in a stack on a warmed plate and cover with a clean tea towel.

Serve hot with butter, if using.

This breakfast is packed full of flavour, as well as nutritious meat and veggies to get your morning started. Although, it has to be said, it makes a pretty great lunch or dinner, too . . .

TEX-MEX BREAKFAST QUESADILLA

Serves 4 as a breakfast/light meal, or 2 as a main

- 2 tbsp olive oil or other cooking fat
- 1 small brown onion, diced
- 1–2 jalapeños, finely diced
- 1 capsicum, diced
- 1 clove garlic, minced
- 300 g beef or pork mince
- ½ tsp chilli powder
- 1 tsp ground cumin
- 1 cup chopped white mushrooms
- 1 large tomato (or two small), diced
- 6 eggs
- salt and pepper to taste
- 4 Primal Tortillas (page 147)
- sprinkle of freshly grated cheese (optional)
- lime or lemon wedges to serve (optional)

Preheat oven to 200°C. Lightly grease a baking sheet, or line with non-stick paper.

Heat olive oil or other cooking fat in a large frying-pan over a medium-high heat. Add onion, jalapeño, capsicum and garlic and cook for a few minutes, stirring occasionally, until softened.

Stir in mince, chilli powder and cumin, breaking up the meat as it begins to cook. Once it is nearly cooked through, stir in mushrooms and tomato.

Whisk eggs together in a small dish, then pour over the top of the mince and veggie mixture. Stir to combine, and cook eggs through to desired doneness (I prefer mine a bit soft). Add salt and pepper to taste.

Fill each tortilla with a few spoonfuls of scramble mixture, then top with a sprinkle of grated cheese if you like. Fold each tortilla in half over the filling and place on the baking sheet.

Bake in the oven for 10–12 minutes, to melt the cheese and crisp up the tortillas.

Serve hot with Sarah's Top Secret Guacamole (page 158) and lime or lemon wedges, if using.

It's said that the mark of a great chef is his (or her!) ability to make a perfect omelette. If that's true, then this recipe is a mark of my laziness at breakfast time. When I can't be bothered assembling the perfect omelette, I just take all the great ingredients of my favourite omelette and scramble them together. And you know what? It's still totally delicious.

THE LAZY COOK'S BREAKFAST SCRAMBLE

Serves 2

5 eggs

¼ cup crumbled feta or other favourite cheese

4 slices bacon, cut into chunks

large handful of fresh baby spinach leaves

salt and pepper to taste

Heat a large frying-pan over a medium-high heat. While it's heating up, whisk eggs together with the feta in a small bowl and set aside.

Once pan is hot, toss in bacon and cook for a few minutes until almost cooked through, then add spinach. It will cook down quite quickly, so don't worry if your pan looks full!

There's no need to grease your pan at this point – there should be plenty of delicious bacon fat in there by now. Pour in egg and cheese mixture and cook, stirring occasionally, until the eggs reach the desired doneness.

Season to taste with salt and pepper and enjoy your protein packed-breakfast (or lunch, dinner, midnight snack, whatever). It's huge, so is best shared with a bacon-loving friend. Although if you eat it all yourself, no one will ever know . . .

Cook's Note

Be sure to look for bacon that contains no nitrates or preservatives. My favourite is Henderson's Dry Cured Bacon, or Primal Kitchen's own Honey Cured Bacon.

This recipe works great with fresh vegetables, or you can throw in leftovers from last night's dinner to make it even bigger! I just love the way the eggs look coming out of the oven, all nestled in amongst the veggies.

BAKED EGG AND VEGGIE HASH

Serves 2

3 tbsp olive oil
1 onion, diced
2–3 cloves garlic, finely diced
1 small orange kumara, grated
2 tbsp tomato paste
2 cups sliced white mushrooms
2 cups chopped fresh bok choy
¼ cup loosely packed chopped fresh basil
4 eggs
salt and pepper to taste

Preheat oven to 180°C. Grease a suitably sized baking dish.

Heat oil in a frying-pan over a medium heat, then add onion and cook for a minute until it starts to soften.

Stir in garlic, kumara and tomato paste, followed by mushrooms. Cook for a few minutes until mushrooms begin to soften. Stir in bok choy and basil, allowing it just to wilt but not get mushy.

Pour veggie mixture into the greased baking dish, then use a spoon to create four small wells in the veggies for the eggs. Crack an egg into each well, then season the whole dish with salt and pepper.

Bake for about 15–20 minutes, or until eggs are cooked to the desired doneness. Allow to cool slightly before serving.

I have a habit of coming up with recipes specifically to serve as a vessel for goat's cheese; I love the stuff. This is a particularly delicious way to eat it. Plus, this recipe is loaded with protein – it's a great way to start the day!

SMOKED SALMON AND ASPARAGUS FRITTATA WITH GOAT'S CHEESE

Serves 2–3

6 eggs

½ cup full-fat milk

¼ cup thinly sliced fresh basil leaves

salt and pepper to taste

1 tbsp butter

3 small shallots, thinly sliced

15 stalks asparagus, tough ends trimmed away

80 g smoked salmon pieces

⅓ cup Creamy Goat's Cheese (page 150)

Preheat the oven grill to 220°C.

Whisk eggs, milk, basil, salt and pepper together. Set aside.

Melt butter in a non-stick ovenproof frying-pan over a medium heat. Add shallots and cook for a few minutes, stirring, allowing them to turn golden and caramelised. Add asparagus and sauté until tender but still crisp, about 3–4 minutes.

Pour egg mixture over the vegetables in the pan, then scatter salmon pieces over the top. Allow to cook for a few minutes until the eggs start to set.

Crumble cheese on top, then lower heat to medium-low and cook for about 2 minutes, until the eggs are almost set but the top is still a little runny.

Place the pan under the grill and allow to cook for about 4–5 minutes, until the top is set and golden brown.

Remove from oven and allow the frittata to stand for a few minutes before cutting and serving.

Cook's Note

If you are not keen on salmon, this recipe is equally delicious made using bacon or leftover cooked chicken in its place.

I love baking food inside other food. It's like making an edible bowl. Luckily, nature provides the perfect veggies for this – in this case, the perfect fungus! What could be better than a bowl you can eat?

PORTOBELLO EGG BAKE WITH WILTED KALE AND HOMEMADE TOMATO SAUCE

Serves 2–3

6 large portobello mushrooms

3–4 tbsp olive oil, plus 1 tbsp extra

1 tsp dried thyme

1 tsp dried basil

½ tsp dried oregano

salt and pepper to taste

6 eggs

2 loosely packed cups chopped fresh kale

1 recipe Primal Tomato Sauce (page 156)

Preheat oven to 200°C. Lightly grease a roasting pan, or line with non-stick paper.

Remove stems and 'ribs' from the mushrooms to leave room for the eggs, and lay mushrooms stem side up on the baking sheet. Drizzle mushrooms with the 3–4 tablespoons of olive oil, and sprinkle thyme, basil and oregano into the mushroom cavities, distributing the herbs evenly. Season each mushroom with salt and pepper.

Bake mushrooms for 10–12 minutes until partially cooked and beginning to brown. Remove from oven.

Carefully crack an egg into each mushroom cavity. Return the pan to the oven to bake for another 8–10 minutes, or until the eggs are cooked to the desired doneness.

While the eggs cook, heat the remaining tablespoon of olive oil in a pan over a medium-high heat. Toss in the chopped kale and cook, stirring occasionally, until the kale has wilted, 3–4 minutes. Remove from the heat.

To serve, top each egg with a few spoonfuls of wilted kale and homemade tomato sauce.

I used to make date scones by the dozen when I worked as an early-morning baker, and I never got tired of it! I love dates. I love scones. I just had to primal-ise them. These scones make a lovely breakfast treat or are perfect for afternoon tea.

DATE SCONES

Makes 10

- ⅓ cup chopped dates
- 1 cup Orange Kumara Purée (page 149)
- 3 eggs
- 2 tbsp liquid honey or pure maple syrup
- 1 tsp Vanilla Extract (page 168)
- 2 tbsp melted butter
- ½ cup coconut flour
- 1 tsp baking soda
- 1 tsp baking powder
- ¼ tsp salt
- 2 tsp cinnamon

Preheat oven to 170°C. Lightly grease a baking sheet, or line with non-stick paper.

Place chopped dates in a bowl and cover with boiling water to soak for a few minutes while you prepare the other ingredients.

Whisk kumara purée, eggs, honey or maple syrup, vanilla and melted butter together. In a separate bowl, sift coconut flour, baking soda, baking powder, salt and cinnamon together.

Combine kumara mixture and flour mixture together and stir well. Strain the water from the chopped dates, and stir dates into the scone batter.

Use a big spoon to drop mounds of the thick batter on the baking sheet, a few centimetres apart.

Bake for 15–20 minutes, until golden brown. Serve warm with butter, or with Apple–Pear Compote (page 166).

Cook's Note

For a dairy-free version, use melted coconut oil in place of the butter.

I discovered this magical recipe by accident one rainy day. I was really hungry but didn't have much in the refrigerator, and sure as hell didn't want to walk to the market in the rain. So I pulled out some of my standard primal baking ingredients, threw them in a bowl and stuck the concoction in the microwave. The result was my favourite primal muffin recipe to date – which is also nut free. You've probably seen many 'microwave cake' recipes before, but most of them are pretty terrible. This one, my friends, is a winner.

MUFFIN IN A MUG

Serves 1–2

1 egg
1 tbsp honey or Date Paste (page 164)
¼ tsp Vanilla Extract (page 168)
1 tbsp melted butter or coconut oil
3 tbsp coconut flour
1 tbsp ground linseed
½ tsp ground cinnamon
¼ tsp baking soda
dash of salt
2 tbsp sultanas

Whisk egg, honey or Date Paste, vanilla and butter or coconut oil together.

In a separate bowl, combine coconut flour, ground linseed, cinnamon, baking soda and salt.

Combine all of the ingredients, stirring in the sultanas last.

Spoon the mixture into two mugs (or one if you're really hungry and don't want to share!) and microwave on high for about 1½ minutes, depending on the power of your microwave.

These muffins make a delicious snack or breakfast on the go. They also freeze really well, so you can make a batch and freeze half for later. You can add in any favourite flavour combination you want, like chopped apple, raisins, blueberries or, for an extra treat, dark chocolate. (Apple is my personal favourite!)

BANANA STREUSEL MUFFINS

Makes 12 medium-sized muffins

Streusel Topping

½ cup chopped walnuts

¼ cup almond flour

1 tsp ground cinnamon

1 tbsp melted butter or coconut oil

Muffins

1½ cups almond flour

1 tsp baking powder

1 tsp baking soda

1 tsp ground cinnamon

¼ tsp salt

3 eggs

¼ cup Date Paste (page 164) or liquid honey

1 cup mashed over-ripe bananas

1 tsp Vanilla Extract (page 168)

Preheat oven to 170°C. Line a 12-hole muffin pan with paper liners, or use melted butter or coconut oil to grease it.

For the Streusel Topping, stir all ingredients together in a bowl and set aside.

For the muffins, in a large bowl mix almond flour, baking powder, baking soda, cinnamon and salt together. Set aside.

In a separate large bowl, whisk eggs, Date Paste or honey, banana and vanilla together.

Add the flour mixture to the banana mixture and stir well to combine.

Scoop batter into prepared muffin cups, filling each three-quarters full. Sprinkle the tops of the muffins with streusel mix. Bake for 20–25 minutes until golden. Allow muffins to cool slightly in the pan, then transfer them to a cooling rack.

These muffins are loaded with goodness. They're also pretty dense, so even if baked in smaller muffin pans they'll keep you full until lunchtime. You can use your favourite combination of veggies for these, or just grab whatever you've got in the refrigerator.

HEARTY SAVOURY MUFFINS

Makes 12 medium-sized muffins

⅔ cup coconut flour
½ cup ground linseed
½ tsp baking soda
½ tsp baking powder
½ tsp salt
½ tsp ground pepper
dash of cayenne pepper
6 eggs
4 tbsp melted butter or coconut oil
1 tomato, diced
1 small courgette, grated or finely diced
½ cup chopped spinach
½ cup grated tasty cheese or crumbled feta (optional)

Preheat oven to 170°C. Line a 12-hole muffin pan with paper liners, or use melted butter or coconut oil to grease it.

Mix coconut flour, ground linseed, baking soda, baking powder, salt, pepper and cayenne pepper together in a large bowl.

In a separate large bowl, whisk eggs and melted butter or coconut oil together, then stir in the flour mixture. Stir in the veggies and cheese, if using.

Scoop mix into prepared muffin cups, filling each three-quarters full. Bake for 12–15 minutes until cooked through, then cool completely in the pan.

Zucchini is, of course, just the American name for courgettes . . . and I know, whatever the name, these muffins sound a bit strange. Chocolate and courgettes? Really? Actually, they're a great sneaky way to get extra greens into your diet. You can't really taste the courgettes – they just make the muffins extra moist. Go ahead, give it a try!

CHOCOLATE ZUCCHINI MUFFINS

Makes 12 medium-sized muffins

4 eggs
⅓ cup liquid honey
1 tsp Vanilla Extract (page 168)
2 over-ripe bananas, mashed
1 cup almond flour
½ cup coconut flour
¼ cup ground linseed
¼ cup cocoa powder, sifted
1 tsp ground cinnamon
2 tsp baking soda
1 tsp baking powder
¼ tsp salt
1 cup grated courgette (about 2 medium-sized courgettes)
½ cup dark chocolate chips (at least 70% cocoa solids)

Preheat oven to 170°C. Line a 12-hole muffin tray with paper liners, or use melted butter or coconut oil to grease it.

Whisk eggs, honey, vanilla and mashed bananas together in a large bowl.

In a separate bowl, stir almond flour, coconut flour, ground linseed, cocoa powder, cinnamon, baking soda, baking powder and salt together.

Whisk flour mixture into banana mixture, then fold in grated courgette and chocolate chips.

Scoop mix into prepared muffin cups, filling each three-quarters full. Bake for 12–15 minutes, until cooked through. Allow to cool completely in the pan.

Main Events

Primal-friendly meals your friends and family will love

This delicious autumn soup will warm you right up, and it freezes well so you can make a large batch and save some for another day.

BUTTERNUT SQUASH AND SAGE SOUP

Serves 4–6

2 tbsp olive oil

1 carrot, peeled and diced

1 celery stalk, diced

1 onion, diced

3 cloves garlic, finely diced

½ tsp ground black pepper

¼ cup loosely packed fresh sage leaves, roughly chopped

1 large or 2 small butternut squash, peeled, de-seeded and cut into small chunks

4 cups Chicken Stock (page 154)

1 cup cream (or coconut cream for dairy-free)

salt and pepper to taste

chopped fresh parsley to garnish (optional)

Heat oil in a large soup pot over a medium heat. Add carrot, celery, onion, garlic, black pepper and sage. Cook until vegetables have begun to soften and onion turns translucent.

Stir in butternut and stock. Bring to a boil, reduce heat and simmer until butternut is cooked through, about 30 minutes.

Purée the soup using a stick blender or food processor, then strain through a sieve. Whisk in the cream, and season to taste with salt and pepper. Garnish with parsley, if using.

I love this soup because it's full of flavour and its main ingredient – the noble carrot – is one of the cheapest vegetables you can get. It makes for a dinner that's not only delicious, but economical too. And like any soup, it tastes even better the day after you make it!

CURRIED CARROT AND GINGER SOUP

Serves 4–6

- 2 tbsp coconut oil (or other cooking fat)
- 2 onions, diced
- 2 tbsp grated fresh ginger
- 2 tbsp curry powder
- 1 tsp cayenne pepper (use more or less to taste)
- 2 tsp turmeric
- ½ tsp ground white pepper
- 1 kg carrots, peeled and diced
- 4 cups Chicken Stock (page 154)
- 1 cup coconut cream
- salt and freshly ground black pepper to taste
- coriander to garnish
- crème fraîche, to serve (optional)

Heat coconut oil or other cooking fat in a large pot over a medium heat, and add onion and ginger. Cook for a few minutes to soften. Add curry powder, cayenne, turmeric and white pepper, and cook for 1 minute more.

Stir carrot in, pour stock in and bring to a simmer. Keep the soup at a low simmer for about 30 minutes, or until the carrots are cooked and quite soft.

Remove the pot from the heat and use a stick blender or food processor to purée the soup until very smooth. Whisk coconut cream in, and continue to whisk or purée until combined. Season to taste with salt. Serve with freshly ground black pepper, coriander and a dollop of crème fraîche, if using.

I used to work in a café where occasionally I would have to make corn fritters for the lunch menu. I can still feel the burn of those exploding kernels as they burst in the hot oil, out of the pan and into my face. The lesson from this? Corn is dangerous. Healthy, tasty paleo fritters are the way to go – no corn necessary!

VEGGIE FRITTERS

Serves 4

- 2–3 medium-sized courgettes
- 1 eggplant
- 2 carrots
- 1 tsp salt
- 1 tsp ground pepper
- 1 brown onion, finely diced
- 3 tbsp chopped fresh parsley
- 1 clove garlic, finely diced
- 3 eggs, lightly beaten
- ¼ cup coconut flour
- ¼ cup almond flour
- 2–4 tbsp olive oil or coconut oil
- fresh parsely to garnish (optional)
- lemon wedges to serve (optional)

Using a large-holed grater, grate courgettes, eggplant and carrots into a large bowl. Stir in salt, pepper, onion, parsley, garlic and eggs. Mix well to combine. Slowly add coconut flour and almond flour, stirring so that no clumps form.

Heat oil in a large frying-pan over a medium-high heat until very hot. Spoon heaped tablespoons of the fritter mixture into the pan, a few inches apart.

Cook the fritters for 2–3 minutes on one side, then flip and continue cooking for another minute on the other side.

Transfer fritters to a plate and continue cooking the rest of the batter, adding more oil to the pan as needed.

Serve garnished with fresh parsley and lemon wedges, if using.

I used to get teased at work for eating salad for lunch every day. And I really did eat it every single day. We nicknamed it the Kitchen Sink Salad, because that's exactly what's in it. I'll generally take whatever tasty veggies I've got on hand, some kind of protein and an easy vinaigrette, throw it on top of some baby spinach, and there's lunch. It's a great way to use leftovers up. By the time I'm done, it tends to be pretty monstrous, but it's full of nothing but healthy goodness. It's primal perfection! You can easily add ingredients to this recipe to dish up lunch for a whole family.

KITCHEN SINK SALAD

Serves 1

- sliced orange or yellow capsicum
- a few cherry tomatoes, halved
- ½ ripe avocado, diced
- grated carrot
- leftovers of whatever protein you had for dinner (chicken, steak, fish, hard-boiled egg . . . it's all good)
- crumbled feta
- diced dates or dried cherries
- great big handful of fresh baby spinach or mesclun
- homemade salad dressing (see options on pages 160–161)

Toss everything together in a bowl. Eat.

This is a great entrée to make in the summertime. It sounds fancy, but is so simple to make. You can swap in your favourite fish, or use whatever looks freshest in the market that day.

SUMMER SEAFOOD CEVICHE

Serves 4

250 g snapper fillets, finely diced

250 g raw prawns (tails removed), peeled and finely diced

250 g raw scallops, finely diced

1 cup lemon juice

½ cup lime juice

2 shallots, finely diced

2 cloves garlic, finely diced

1 hot chilli, finely diced

½ cup chopped fresh coriander

2 vine-ripened tomatoes, diced

½ cucumber, diced

salt and pepper to taste

butterhead lettuce (or other soft lettuce leaves)

1–2 ripe avocados, sliced

Place snapper, prawns and scallops in a shallow dish. Combine lemon and lime juices, shallots, garlic and chilli, and pour this over the fish, covering it completely. The acid in the citrus will 'cook' the fish while you prepare the other ingredients. This is why the seafood needs to be chopped small. Let it sit for about 45 minutes to an hour, until the prawns are pink and the fish is opaque (cooked-looking).

Drain the seafood mixture and combine with coriander, tomatoes and cucumber. Toss gently and season to taste with salt and pepper.

Serve spooned over soft lettuce with sliced avocado on top.

This recipe is my tribute to shrimp 'n' grits – a classic American dish from the South made with Gulf shrimp and coarse cornmeal grits. My version is much better for you and just as delicious!

SPICY CAJUN PRAWNS WITH SIMPLE CAULIFLOWER PURÉE

Serves 4

- 1 tsp ground cumin
- 1 tsp ground coriander
- 1 tsp paprika
- 1 tsp dried oregano
- ½ tsp salt
- ½ tsp freshly ground black pepper
- ½–1 tsp chilli powder
- 750 g raw prawns, peeled, tails on
- juice of 1 lime
- 3 spring onions, thinly sliced
- coconut oil or olive oil as needed
- Simple Cauliflower Purée (page 149), to serve
- 1–2 avocados, sliced, to serve
- Pineapple Chutney (page 169), to serve

Combine cumin, coriander, paprika, oregano, salt, pepper and chilli powder (use more or less to taste, depending on how spicy you like it).

Toss prawns in the spice mixture and add lime juice and spring onion.

Heat a frying-pan over a medium-high heat and add a few tablespoons of coconut or olive oil. Once hot, add prawns and spring onion (reserving some for garnish) and cook, stirring occasionally. The prawns should only need a few minutes to cook, depending on the size.

Remove prawns to a serving platter. Serve hot over Simple Cauliflower Purée garnished with spring onion and with slices of fresh avocado and some Pineapple Chutney on the side.

I've said it before . . . I can be a pretty lazy cook, so my favourite way to prepare fish is to do almost nothing to it. I love snapper, but you can use any kind of fish you like, or just whatever is fresh at the market that day. I discovered fish tacos at the incredible Cabo Fish Taco in Blacksburg, Virginia, while studying at Virginia Tech University. I ate them all the time and they're still one of my favourite foods. The best part is that they need almost no modifications to primal-ise them! They're super-healthy and satisfying, and who doesn't like food you can eat with your hands?

FISH TACOS WITH FRESH MANGO SALSA

Serves 4

1 whole snapper, gutted and scaled (the guy at the market can do this for you)

2–3 tbsp olive oil

salt and pepper to taste

1 recipe Primal Tortillas (page 147)

¼ green cabbage, thinly sliced, to serve

Fresh Mango Salsa

2 ripe mangos, peeled, pitted and diced

½ a medium-sized red onion, finely chopped

1 jalapeño, finely diced

1 small cucumber, diced

¼ cup chopped fresh coriander leaves

2 tbsp fresh lime juice

2 tbsp fresh lemon juice

salt and pepper to taste

To make the Fresh Mango Salsa, combine all the ingredients in a bowl.

Rinse and dry the fish inside and out.

Light your barbecue, and while it's heating up use a very sharp knife to cut a few shallow slits into the sides of the fish. Drizzle oil over the whole fish, and season with salt and pepper.

Lay the fish on the grill and cook for about 5–10 minutes per side, until done (this will depend on the size of your fish). If you don't have a grill, you can do this easily under the grill in your oven. Set fish aside to cool slightly before serving.

To serve, tear fish into large chunks then fill Primal Tortillas with a few pieces of fish, a spoonful of Fresh Mango Salsa and some sliced cabbage.

Cook's Note

These are great with guacamole as well! If you're watching your carbs, you can use lettuce leaves instead of tortillas to wrap your taco filling in.

These are delicious and really quick and easy to throw together. I love to eat them with a fried egg on top. Who needs hash browns?

KUMARA SALMON CAKES

Serves 2

1 medium-sized orange kumara, peeled and cubed
200 g canned salmon
¼ cup coconut flour
¼ cup almond flour
2 eggs
2 spring onions, chopped
juice of ½ lemon
½ tsp salt
½ tsp ground black pepper
coconut oil as needed
Paleo Aïoli (page 155), to serve
salad leaves, to serve
lemon wedges, to serve

Place kumara in a saucepan of cold water and bring to a boil, then turn down to a simmer and cook until soft. Cool, then mash until smooth.

Stir in salmon, coconut flour, almond flour, eggs, spring onion, lemon juice, salt and pepper. Form the mixture into small patties.

Heat a few teaspoons of coconut oil in a frying-pan over a medium-high heat. Once hot, lay the patties in the pan, a few at a time, and cook for about 5 minutes per side.

Serve warm with Paleo Aïoli, salad leaves and lemon wedges on the side.

Classic basil and pine nut pesto is delicious, but I like to add different herbs and nuts to the mixture to make it a bit more interesting. Here, the bright flavour of the basil and rocket paired with the fish and asparagus really brings together all the tastes of spring!

BAKED TARAKIHI WITH LEMON AND OLIVES

Serves 4

4 tarakihi fillets (or other white fish)

1 tbsp olive oil

¼ cup Fresh Herb Pesto (page 162), plus extra to serve

¼ cup sliced black olives

juice of 1 lemon

salt and pepper to taste

Brown Butter Asparagus

2 small bunches of asparagus

3 tbsp butter

salt and pepper to taste

Preheat oven to 200°C. Lightly grease a baking dish, or line with non-stick paper.

Arrange fish in the baking dish and top each piece with a drizzle of olive oil, some pesto, a few olives and a squeeze of lemon juice. Season with salt and pepper and bake for 15 minutes or until fish is cooked.

Meanwhile, trim the tough ends off the asparagus and discard. Bring a large pot of water to a boil and blanch the asparagus spears by dropping them into the boiling water for just 2 minutes, then immediately removing them to a bowl of iced water to stop the cooking. Once cooled, drain the asparagus and pat it dry.

Heat butter in a large frying-pan over a medium heat. Cook the butter for a few minutes until it bubbles and starts to brown. Add in the asparagus and toss it through the brown butter to coat. Season to taste with salt and pepper.

Serve the tarakihi with the Brown Butter Asparagus alongside.

This is another great recipe using my Primal Tortillas. These hot, spicy enchiladas served up with cool, fresh Pico de Gallo is a winning combination.

CHICKEN ENCHILADAS WITH FRESH PICO DE GALLO

Serves 3–4

Enchiladas

2 tbsp olive oil

1 small brown onion, diced

1 red capsicum, diced

3 cloves garlic, finely diced

1 tsp salt

½ tsp freshly ground black pepper

1 tsp chilli powder

1 tsp ground coriander

1 tsp ground cumin

500 g chicken tenderloins, cut into small chunks

1 can (400 g) diced tomatoes

1 large handful of fresh baby spinach

1 cup shredded tasty cheese, plus extra for topping (optional)

1 recipe Primal Tortillas (page 147)

Pico de Gallo

1 small red onion, diced

2 jalapeños, finely diced (remove seeds for a milder flavour)

2 cloves garlic, finely diced

5 vine-ripened tomatoes, diced

½ cup loosely packed chopped fresh coriander

juice of 1 lime

salt and pepper to taste

To make the Pico de Gallo, stir all ingredients together in a bowl. Season to taste with salt and pepper.

Preheat oven to 180°C. Lightly grease a casserole dish with melted coconut oil or butter.

Heat olive oil in a large frying-pan over a medium heat. Stir in onion and capsicum and cook for 1–2 minutes until beginning to soften. Add the garlic and continue cooking for another minute.

Stir in salt, pepper, chilli powder, coriander and cumin, then add diced chicken to the pan. Cook for 8–10 minutes, stirring occasionally, until chicken is cooked through.

Stir in tomatoes and baby spinach, and cook just until spinach is wilted. Remove pan from heat and allow enchilada filling to cool. Stir in shredded cheese, if using.

Fill each tortilla with a scoop of enchilada filling, roll up and place seam side down into the casserole dish. Top each enchilada with a tablespoon of Pico de Gallo and a sprinkle of cheese, if using, then bake for 15–20 minutes until golden brown and cheese has melted.

Serve warm with more Pico de Gallo.

Chicken is a delicious and easy one-pot dinner. Here's one of my favourite ways to prepare it.

LEMON, GARLIC AND THYME ROASTED CHICKEN AND ROOT VEGGIES

Serves 4

1 whole free-range chicken
2 lemons
salt and pepper as needed
3 cloves garlic, finely diced
3–4 sprigs fresh thyme
2 small orange kumara
2 beetroot, stems removed
2 parsnips, peeled, stems removed
2 carrots, peeled, stems removed
olive oil or melted butter as needed

Preheat oven to 180°C.

Place chicken in a roasting pan. Halve the lemons, squeeze the juice of one lemon over the chicken, then stuff the two lemon shells into the cavity of the chicken.

Sprinkle salt, pepper and garlic over the top of the chicken. Place half the thyme on top of the chicken and the rest inside the chicken cavity.

Chop kumara, beetroot, parsnips and carrots in big chunks (see Cook's Note) and place in the roasting pan alongside the chicken. Drizzle with olive oil or melted butter and juice from the remaining lemon. Season well with salt and pepper.

Cover with aluminium foil and roast for 1 hour. Remove foil and finish cooking for about 20–30 minutes, or until the meat is cooked through.

Cook's Note

Beetroot are famous for taking much longer to cook than other root veggies. I recommend cutting them a bit smaller than the rest of the vegetables to ensure even cooking.

Most people are probably used to being lectured on how the best meat for you is boneless, skinless chicken breast because it contains a lot of protein with the least amount of fat. Well, it also usually contains the least amount of flavour. And since with primal eating fat is now our friend, you should go for the cut of chicken you like best! Cooking meat with the bone in is always best for retaining moisture and flavour. So if you do like to cook chicken breasts, I recommend getting skin-on, bone-in cuts.

MIDDLE EASTERN BRAISED CHICKEN AND 'RICE'

Serves 4

- 1½ kg chicken pieces (breasts, thighs or drumsticks, whatever you like)
- salt and pepper as needed
- 1 tbsp olive oil
- 5 shallots, thinly sliced
- 1 tbsp ground cinnamon
- 2 tsp grated fresh ginger
- 1 tsp ground cumin
- 1 tsp turmeric
- ¼ tsp cayenne pepper (or more to your liking)
- 3 cups Chicken Stock (page 154)
- juice of 1 lemon
- 1 can (425 ml) coconut milk
- 10 dates, chopped
- 10 dried apricots, chopped
- ¼ cup fresh coriander leaves
- ¼ cup sliced almonds, toasted
- 1 recipe Basic Cauliflower Rice (page 146)

Sprinkle chicken pieces with salt and pepper. Heat olive oil in a heavy, deep pan over a medium-high heat. Add chicken pieces to pan and cook, turning, until browned on all sides, then remove to a platter.

Reduce heat to medium, add shallots to pan and sauté until golden, adding more olive oil if needed. Stir in cinnamon, ginger, cumin, turmeric and cayenne pepper and cook for another minute.

Place chicken pieces back in the pan and cover with stock and lemon juice. Bring the liquid to a boil, then reduce to a low simmer for about 25 minutes or until chicken is cooked through.

Transfer chicken and shallots to a platter, add coconut milk to the pan and boil until slightly thickened. Stir in dates and apricots and cook for another 5 minutes.

Pour sauce over chicken and garnish with coriander. Sprinkle almonds over Basic Cauliflower Rice.

Growing up I never liked tomatoes much, until I was a teenager and religiously watched Ina Garten's cooking show *Barefoot Contessa* on TV. One day she made slow-cooked balsamic tomatoes that looked so good I had to try them. She had me hooked and this has been my favourite way to cook tomatoes ever since! Here's my version, set alongside some tasty baked chicken for a delicious meal.

BAKED CHICKEN WITH BALSAMIC ROASTED TOMATOES

Serves 4–6

Tomatoes

10 plum tomatoes, halved lengthwise

4 tbsp olive oil

4 tbsp balsamic vinegar

2 large cloves garlic, finely diced

1 tsp salt

1 tsp freshly ground black pepper

fresh basil, thinly sliced, to serve (optional)

Chicken

¼ cup olive oil

juice of 1 lemon

1 tbsp wholegrain mustard

6 bone-in, skin-on chicken thighs

salt and pepper to taste

salad leaves, to serve

lemon wedges, to serve

Preheat oven to 200°C.

Arrange the tomatoes on a baking tray, cut sides up, in a single layer. Drizzle with olive oil and balsamic vinegar. Sprinkle garlic, salt and pepper over the tomatoes. Roast for 25–30 minutes, until the tomatoes are soft and a bit browned.

Remove from oven, set aside and lower the heat to 180°C.

While the tomatoes are cooking, whisk olive oil, lemon juice and mustard together. Place chicken pieces in a roasting pan, set close together and pour olive oil mixture over the top. Season with salt and pepper.

Roast chicken for about 25–35 minutes, or until cooked through. Serve with salad leaves, lemon wedges and the tomatoes, topped with fresh basil, if using.

This tasty curry tastes even better the day after you make it, if you can wait that long to eat it!

CHICKEN AND PUMPKIN CURRY WITH MANGO CHUTNEY

Serves 4

2 tbsp coconut oil

1 onion, diced

3 cloves garlic, finely diced

1 tbsp grated fresh ginger

1 tbsp turmeric

2 tbsp curry powder

½ tsp chilli flakes

500 g chicken breasts, cut into bite-sized chunks

4 cups fresh pumpkin, peeled, de-seeded and cut into bite-sized chunks

1 cup Chicken Stock (page 154) or vegetable stock

1 cup coconut milk

1 recipe Basic Cauliflower Rice (page 146)

1 bunch fresh coriander, leaves picked, to garnish

Mango Chutney

1 tbsp coconut oil

1 brown onion, diced

2 tbsp grated fresh ginger

2 cloves garlic, finely diced

1 tbsp garam masala

½ tsp chilli flakes

1 tsp salt

½ tsp mustard seeds

2 ripe mangos, pitted, peeled and diced

½ cup Date Paste (page 164)

¾ cup cider vinegar

½ cup sultanas

1 cup water

To make the Mango Chutney, heat oil in a saucepan over a medium heat. Once hot, add onion and cook until beginning to soften, about 3–4 minutes. Stir in ginger, garlic, garam masala, chilli flakes, salt and mustard seeds and continue to cook until fragrant, about 1 minute.

Stir in mango, Date Paste, vinegar, sultanas and water. Bring to a boil, then reduce heat and simmer until mango is soft and sauce is thick and syrupy, about 45–50 minutes.

For the curry, heat oil in a pan over a medium-high heat. Add onion, garlic and ginger and cook until they begin to soften.

Stir in turmeric, curry powder and chilli flakes, followed by the chicken. Cook, stirring occasionally, until chicken is opaque and cooked through, about 7–8 minutes.

Stir in chopped pumpkin, then add stock and coconut milk and simmer over a medium-low heat until pumpkin is cooked, about 20 minutes.

Serve with Basic Cauliflower Rice and Mango Chutney. Garnish with fresh coriander leaves.

Coconut oil is the best frying fat for this particular recipe, as it has a high smoke point and a delicious but mild flavour. This is a great kid-friendly recipe – just tell them it's McDonald's chicken nuggets . . . they might believe you! You might even fool yourself. You definitely won't miss junky fast food once you start making these. Try them with my Sweet and Smoky Boysenberry Barbecue Sauce (page 157) or Paleo Aïoli (page 155).

'BREADED' CHICKEN

Serves 4

- ¾ cup almond flour
- ½ cup coconut flour
- ⅓ cup finely grated Parmesan
- 1 tsp salt
- ½ tsp garlic powder
- ½ tsp ground black pepper
- pinch of cayenne pepper
- 3 eggs
- ¼ cup full-fat milk
- coconut oil for frying
- 1 kg chicken tenderloins
- salad leaves, to serve
- lemon wedges, to serve

Combine almond flour, coconut flour, Parmesan, salt, garlic powder, black pepper and cayenne pepper in a shallow bowl.

In a separate bowl, whisk together the eggs and milk.

Heat a few tablespoons of coconut oil in a frying-pan over a medium-high heat.

Set up a chicken assembly line next to the pan – flour mixture closest, then egg mixture, then chicken. Take each piece of chicken, one at a time, and dip it first in the egg mixture and then in the flour mixture, then place it in the pan. Cook each tenderloin for 3–4 minutes per side, depending on how big they are. (If they're very big, you can cut them in half before cooking.)

Serve hot with salad leaves, lemon wedges and Sweet and Smoky Boysenberry Barbecue Sauce or Paleo Aïoli.

Here I go again, stuffing food with more food – I can't help myself! I think it's just the tastiest way to cook something. In this recipe I use my homemade ricotta cheese. It's easy and fun to do, and sounds really impressive when you tell people you made your own.

STUFFED CHICKEN BREASTS

Serves 4

3–4 rashers honey-cured bacon

300 g white mushrooms, sliced

2 shallots, finely diced

4 free-range chicken breasts

¾ cup ricotta cheese (see Cook's Note on page 150)

¼ cup thinly sliced fresh basil

¼ cup walnuts, toasted and chopped

salt and pepper to taste

olive oil as needed

salad leaves, to serve

Preheat oven to 180°C.

Dice bacon and cook in a large frying-pan over a medium-high heat until crispy. Remove from the pan with a slotted spoon and keep the bacon fat in the pan.

Sauté mushrooms and shallots in the bacon fat until soft, then stir in the cooked bacon and set aside to cool.

Place chicken breasts in a lightly greased baking dish. Using a sharp knife, cut a horizontal slit through each breast, cutting almost all of the way through but without slicing them completely in half, so they will hold the filling.

Once the bacon and mushroom mixture has cooled, fold it into the ricotta with the basil and walnuts, then season the mixture to taste with salt and pepper.

Divide stuffing mixture evenly among the four breasts (they will be very full!). Drizzle the tops of the chicken breasts with a little olive oil, then sprinkle with salt and pepper.

Bake for 25–30 minutes, or until the chicken is cooked through. Serve with salad leaves.

I love the intense flavour of smoked meats, but I don't have the space (or the patience) for a great big meat smoker in my yard. The solution? Liquid smoke. What is that, you ask? Well, it's exactly what it sounds like. All-natural hickory-smoke flavour, concentrated and bottled for everyday kitchen use. It can be found in most specialty grocery stores – you just didn't know to look for it until now! Liquid smoke is ideal for helping make the less glamorous, cheaper cuts of meat like pork shoulder taste out of this world. It's powerful stuff, so you only need a little to give your pork some awesome smoky flavour.

SMOKY SLOW-COOKER PULLED PORK WITH PARSNIP PURÉE

Serves 6

1 free-farmed, bone-in pork shoulder (about 2 kg)

2 cups Chicken Stock (page 154)

¼ cup blackstrap molasses

4 cloves garlic, crushed

1 tsp liquid smoke

Parsnip Purée

3 shallots, diced

2 cloves garlic, finely chopped

50 g butter

500 g parsnips, peeled and cut into chunks

2 cups Chicken Stock (page 154) or vegetable stock

salt and pepper to taste

Place pork shoulder, stock, molasses, garlic and liquid smoke in a slow-cooker. Cook on the low setting for 8–10 hours until meat is falling apart.

To make the Parsnip Purée, gently fry shallots and garlic in butter until soft. Add parsnips and cook for 5 minutes. Add stock, bring to a boil and simmer until the parsnips are soft. Drain, reserving the cooking liquid, and purée in a blender or food processor, adding some of the reserved liquid a little at a time to get a creamy texture. Season to taste with salt and pepper.

Use two forks to shred the meat.

Place the cooking liquid from the pork in a saucepan and simmer until slightly thickened.

Serve pork alongside the Parsnip Purée and spoon over cooking liquid to serve.

Cook's Note

This can also be done in a conventional oven. Simply place all ingredients in a large, heavy casserole with a well-fitting lid – I use a Dutch oven, which is specially designed for slow cooking – cover and cook in a 140°C oven for 3–4 hours until tender.

Thank you for your interest and support for **Primal Kitchen**!

Please help us encourage Amazon.com to carry Sarah's book here in North America. Just send Amazon an inquiry, noting the following

Book Title:	**Primal Kitchen**
Author:	Sarah Dueweke
Published by:	Penguin Books New Zealand
ISBN Number:	978-0-14-357244-2

Spread the word!

My family hails from Northern Michigan, where cooking with cherries is a part of life! And who can resist the delicious, crispy goodness of crackled pork skin?

BRAISED PORK BELLY WITH SWEET CHERRIES

Serves 4

2 sprigs fresh thyme, chopped

2 tsp sea salt

2 tsp Chinese five spice

1 tbsp melted coconut oil

1 kg piece boneless pork belly

1 tbsp olive oil

3 shallots, sliced thinly

3 cloves garlic, sliced thinly

1 bay leaf

1½ cups unsweetened apple juice

1½ cups Chicken Stock (page 154)

½ cup dried cherries

Simple Roasted Pumpkin

½ small pumpkin, peeled and cut into half-moon slices

2–3 tbsp olive oil

salt and pepper to taste

Combine thyme, sea salt, five spice and coconut oil and rub the mixture onto all sides of the pork belly. Cover tightly with plastic wrap and refrigerate overnight.

Preheat oven to 140°C. Remove pork from refrigerator, unwrap and place in a roasting pan.

In a large saucepan, heat olive oil over a medium-high heat. Add shallots and garlic and cook until soft, then add bay leaf and cook for another minute. Pour in apple juice and stock, and bring just to a boil. Remove from the heat and pour into the roasting pan, around the pork belly. Cover the pan with aluminium foil and place in the oven to braise for 3 hours.

Remove pork from oven and turn oven up to 180°C.

Remove pork from the braising liquid and cover with the foil to keep it warm while you cook the pumpkin. Toss pumpkin pieces with olive oil and season generously with salt and pepper. Roast for 30–40 minutes, until slightly crispy on the outside and soft on the inside.

Remove pumpkin from oven and set oven grill to 220°C.

Strain the braising liquid through a sieve into a saucepan, stir in the dried cherries and bring to a simmer. Allow to simmer for 20–25 minutes until reduced and slightly thickened.

Meanwhile, place the pork belly back in the roasting dish and place under the grill for 15–20 minutes, until the skin is deliciously golden, crispy and crackling. You can keep the pumpkin warm on the shelf below.

Serve the pork belly warm with the reduced sauce and cherries, with Simple Roasted Pumpkin and a green salad on the side.

Cook's Notes

Place pumpkin in a hot oven for 5–10 minutes before you cut it up – the skin will soften, making the job much easier.
Look for dried – not glacé – cherries in the baking aisle of the supermarket, with the raisins and other dried fruits.

This recipe reminds me of my dad, because it's one of his favourites. When I was at university and still living at home, Dad was always happy to let me experiment in the kitchen and feed him whatever I came up with. This would be worthy of Frankenmuth, eh Dad?

GERMAN-STYLE SAUSAGES WITH ROASTED CABBAGE, APPLE AND CARAWAY

Serves 3–4

2 tbsp olive oil

2 tbsp malt vinegar

2 tbsp chopped fresh thyme (or 2 tsp dried thyme)

1 tsp caraway seeds

2 medium-sized red onions, thinly sliced

1 small red cabbage, thinly sliced

2 green apples, peeled and cut into wedges

salt and pepper to taste

6 mild pork sausages

Preheat oven to 200°C.

Whisk oil, vinegar, thyme and caraway seeds together in a small bowl.

Combine onion, cabbage and apples in a roasting pan and drizzle with the oil mixture. Stir to coat evenly, then sprinkle generously with salt and pepper. Lay the sausages on top of the mixture.

Roast for 10 minutes, then stir. Continue cooking until cabbage is tender but not mushy, and sausages are done (about another 15 minutes).

Slice sausages and serve with extra malt vinegar if you like.

Cook's Note

Be sure to look for a brand of sausages that has no added sugars or gluten.

The capsicum . . . another delicious farmers' market find that can be used as a vessel to hold more food! I like to make this recipe with the most colourful capsicums I can find. They're so sweet and just look beautiful when you cook them. Fun fact – an orange capsicum has even more vitamin C than an orange! Another reason to cook this dish up straight away.

MEATY STUFFED CAPSICUMS

Serves 6 (or 4 very hungry people)

- 6 medium-sized colourful capsicums
- 3 tbsp olive oil, plus extra as needed
- 1 brown onion, diced
- 2 cloves garlic, finely diced
- 1 tsp dried thyme
- 2 tsp dried oregano
- 500 g minced beef
- 1 cup sliced mushrooms
- 2 courgettes, diced
- 1 small eggplant, diced
- 1 can (400 g) diced tomatoes, drained (or use fresh)
- 2 tbsp tomato paste
- 1 cup fresh rocket or chopped spinach
- ¾ cup crumbled feta (optional)
- salt and pepper to taste

Preheat oven to 180°C.

Cut tops off capsicums, reserving the 'lids', and remove seeds and ribs from the insides. Stand capsicums up in a casserole dish and set aside.

Heat olive oil in a large pan over a medium-high heat. Add onion and cook for a few minutes, until soft. Stir in garlic, thyme and oregano, cook for a minute longer, then add beef. Break up the meat as it cooks, stirring occasionally.

When the meat is nearly cooked, stir in mushrooms, courgettes, eggplant and tomatoes and continue to cook until the vegetables are tender. Stir in tomato paste, followed by rocket or spinach.

Remove from heat and stir in feta, if using. Season to taste with salt and pepper.

Spoon meat mixture into the capsicums and place the 'lids' back on top. Drizzle the tops with olive oil and sprinkle with salt and pepper, then bake until the capsicums are soft and a bit browned, about 30–40 minutes.

Luckily for me red wine is primal, because I love cooking with it – especially when it's cold outside. Using short ribs and cooking them low and slow will give you that mouth-watering, fall-off-the-bone meat you'll have people drooling over! If you want to make a pure paleo version of this recipe, you can easily substitute the red wine with additional beef or chicken stock.

RED WINE BRAISED SHORT RIBS WITH SAUTÉED MUSHROOMS AND LEEK

Serves 4

1 kg bone-in beef short ribs

salt and pepper to taste

3 tbsp olive oil, plus extra

1 onion, diced

1 carrot, peeled and diced

2 stalks celery, diced

2 cloves garlic, finely diced

2 tbsp tomato paste

2 cups dry red wine

2 cups beef or Chicken Stock (page 154)

3 sprigs fresh thyme

1 sprig fresh rosemary

1 bay leaf

1 recipe Golden Kumara Mash (page 148), to serve

Sautéed Mushrooms and Leek

1 small leek

3 tbsp butter

3 cloves garlic, finely diced

500 g white mushrooms, washed and thinly sliced

salt and pepper to taste

Season the ribs on all sides with salt and pepper.

In a large, heavy pot, heat olive oil over a medium-high heat. Add ribs to the pot and cook, turning, until browned on all sides, then remove to a plate.

Add an additional tablespoon of olive oil to the pot. Stir in onion, carrot, celery and garlic and cook over a moderate heat, stirring occasionally, until softened and lightly browned. Stir in tomato paste. Add wine and stock, scraping the bottom of the pot with a wooden spoon to get off any bits of meat that may have stuck. Add thyme, rosemary and bay leaf and bring to a simmer.

Return the ribs to the pot. Partially cover and cook over a moderately low heat, just above a simmer, until very tender, about 2½–3 hours.

Transfer the ribs to a plate, then strain the sauce through a sieve. Return the sauce to the pot and boil until reduced by half, about 10 minutes.

Meanwhile, cut the stalky green end from the leek and discard, then cut the white part into thin slices.

Heat butter in a frying-pan over a medium heat until hot. Add garlic and cook for 1–2 minutes, until fragrant. Stir in mushrooms and leek and cook, stirring occasionally, until softened. Season to taste with salt and pepper.

Return the meat to the sauce and simmer over a low heat until heated through. Serve with the Sautéed Mushrooms and Leek and Golden Kumara Mash.

Fact: I braise meat, a lot. If you're on a budget, you have to know how to cook cheaper cuts of meat so that they're still tender and delicious, and braising is the way to do it! For primal/paleo people, a slow-cooker can be your best friend, but if you don't have one don't worry – this works just as well in the oven. Shins sound like a weird thing to eat, but they are fantastic! I look for the ones with thick bones for lots of flavour, and so that I can scoop out the marrow to eat at the end – it tastes incredible spread on my Primal Dinner Rolls.

BRAISED BEEF SHINS WITH ROASTED BRUSSELS SPROUTS AND PRIMAL DINNER ROLLS

Serves 4

- 3 tbsp olive oil, plus more as needed
- 1½ kg beef shins
- salt and pepper to taste
- 2 large onions, diced
- 2 large stalks celery, cut into chunks
- 2 carrots, diced
- 4 cloves garlic, crushed
- 1 kg white mushrooms, washed and cut into 1 cm pieces
- 2 tbsp tomato paste
- 2 tbsp paprika
- 2 cups beef stock
- 1 recipe Primal Dinner Rolls (see page 146)

Roasted Brussels Sprouts

- 500 g fresh Brussels sprouts
- 3–4 tbsp melted butter or bacon fat
- salt and pepper to taste
- ¼ cup chopped pecans

Preheat oven to 160°C.

Heat oil in a large frying-pan over a medium-high heat. Season beef shins well with salt and pepper. Add the meat to the pan to brown on all sides, then remove to a large, heavy casserole (I use a Dutch oven) or slow-cooker.

Add a bit more oil to the pan, then add onion, celery, carrot and garlic and cook, stirring, until the onion is soft and beginning to brown. Add mushrooms and cook until beginning to soften. Stir in tomato paste and paprika, then remove from the heat.

Spread the sautéed vegetable mixture over the beef shins and add beef stock. The beef should be completely submerged in liquid; if not, add water as needed.

Place the lid on the casserole and bake until beef is very tender, 3–3½ hours. If using a slow-cooker, cook on low for 6–8 hours.

Transfer beef and mushrooms to a platter with a slotted spoon, then strain the cooking liquid into a saucepan. Bring to a simmer and reduce to thicken.

Preheat oven to 200°C for the Brussels sprouts. Cut ends off sprouts and remove outer leaves. Cut sprouts in half and place in a casserole dish. Toss sprouts in melted butter or bacon fat and sprinkle with salt and pepper.

Roast for about 20 minutes. Stir in chopped pecans, then cook for another 15 minutes or until pecans are golden and slightly crisp on the outside.

Season the reduced sauce to taste with salt and pepper, then stir beef and mushrooms back into the sauce. The meat will be tender and falling off the bones. Serve with Roasted Brussels Sprouts and Primal Dinner Rolls.

Meatloaf is a great make-ahead dish. I often double the recipe, then freeze one to have on hand for a day when I'm too busy (er . . . lazy) to cook.

MEATLOAF WITH SWEET AND SMOKY BOYSENBERRY BARBECUE SAUCE

Serves 4–6

2 tbsp butter or olive oil
1 clove garlic, finely diced
1 brown onion, finely chopped
1 carrot, grated
1 courgette, grated
300 g white mushrooms, chopped small
½ tsp dried oregano
¼ tsp dried thyme
½ tsp salt
¼ tsp black pepper
500 g minced beef
500 g minced pork
2 eggs, whisked
Sweet and Smoky Boysenberry Barbecue Sauce (page 157), to serve

Preheat oven to 180°C.

Heat butter or olive oil in a large frying-pan over a medium heat. Toss in garlic, onion, carrot, courgette and mushrooms, and cook for a few minutes until softened. Set aside to cool. Stir in oregano, thyme, salt and pepper.

In a large bowl, combine minced meats and egg with the cooled vegetables. You can use a spoon, but it's easier to mash it up with your hands.

Lightly grease a loaf pan and fill it with the meatloaf mixture. Spread a layer of Sweet and Smoky Boysenberry Barbecue Sauce on top, then put in the oven to bake for about an hour.

Allow to cool slightly before cutting into it. Serve with more Sweet and Smoky Boysenberry Barbecue Sauce on the side.

One of my favourite foods as a kid was stuffed jacket potatoes, loaded with cheese and sour cream and other heavy, greasy stuff. This version is made with beef, vegetables and herbs to make a hearty, filling meal that you can feel really good about eating.

COMFORTING STUFFED KUMARA

Serves 4

- 3 tbsp butter or coconut oil
- 3 medium-sized red kumara
- salt and pepper to taste
- 1 brown onion, diced
- 1 clove garlic, finely diced
- 500 g minced beef
- 1 tsp dried basil
- 1 tsp dried oregano
- 1 tbsp tomato paste
- 1 cup loosely packed chopped raw spinach
- ¾ cup grated tasty cheese (optional)

Preheat oven to 200°C.

Rub half of the butter or coconut oil all over the kumara, sprinkle with a bit of salt, then cut in half lengthwise. Place cut side down on a baking sheet and bake for about 25–30 minutes until cooked through.

While the kumara bake, heat a large frying-pan over a medium-high heat. Add remaining butter or coconut oil to the pan and, once hot, add in onion and garlic.

When the onion begins to soften, stir minced beef in, breaking it up with a wooden spoon as it cooks. Stir in basil, oregano and tomato paste. When the beef mixture is nearly cooked, stir spinach in and continue cooking until just wilted.

Once the kumara are done, pull them out of the oven and let them cool for a few minutes before carefully spooning out the insides into a large bowl. Leave the kumara-skin 'shells' on the baking sheet.

Mash the kumara flesh well, then stir in the meat mixture and grated cheese, if using. Season to taste with salt and pepper. Re-stuff the kumara skins with the filling and place them back in the oven on the top rack to cook for another 3–5 minutes or until the cheese has melted and/or the tops are golden.

Cook's Note

I find red kumara is best for this recipe, as the skin is a little bit tougher than orange kumara, making it better able to hold the filling.

Who needs a bun? Without it, you've got more room for delicious burger toppings. It's like playing Jenga with your food. I enjoy topping most of my food with a runny egg anyway. It's my inner Anthony Bourdain coming out.

BUN-LESS KIWI BURGER STACK WITH BAKED KUMARA WEDGES

Serves 4

Patties

1 kg minced lamb

1 small brown onion, finely diced

3 cloves garlic, finely diced

1 tsp ground cumin

1 tsp paprika

1 tsp salt

½ tsp ground black pepper

¼ cup coconut flour

¼ cup finely chopped fresh parsley

1 egg

To Serve (any quantities you like)

Fermented Beetroot (page 152)

nitrate-free bacon

fresh tomato, sliced

fried eggs

fresh avocado, sliced

baby lettuce leaves

Baked Kumara Wedges (page 148)

Paleo Aïoli (page 155)

Combine all ingredients for the burger patties, mixing well. (This job is best done with your hands! Just be sure to wash them before giving someone a high-five . . .) Shape into 4–5 patties and fire up the barbecue (or heat a stovetop grill pan) to medium-high heat.

Lightly grease the barbecue grill or pan, then cook the lamb patties for about 4–5 minute per side, or slightly less if you like a pink centre.

Serve up the burgers stacked with your favourite fixin's – beetroot, bacon, tomato, egg, avocado, lettuce . . . Don't forget the Baked Kumara Wedges and Paleo Aïoli!

When I was at university, I briefly worked at a 24-hour Greek diner. The hours were long, the pay was awful, but the food was amazing. They made tzatziki sauce by the vat – it was incredible how much they went through! I loved the stuff and luckily for me it's totally primal. Here's a delicious way to eat it, perfect for the barbecue.

GREEK LAMB SKEWERS WITH TZATZIKI SAUCE

Serves 4

1 kg diced lamb (leg meat works well)

3 colourful capsicums, cut into large chunks

1 eggplant, cut into 3–4 cm cubes

1 medium red onion, cut into large chunks

¼ cup olive oil

salt and pepper to taste

Tzatziki Sauce

1 large cucumber

1½ cups thick Greek yoghurt

2–3 cloves garlic, finely diced

1 tbsp lemon juice

salt and pepper to taste

To make the Tzatziki Sauce, grate the cucumber (on the large-holed side of the grater) and place in a sieve over an empty bowl. Sprinkle with a bit of salt – this will draw out the liquid and ensure a thicker, creamy sauce instead of a watery one. Allow to drain for at least 30 minutes while you prepare your lamb skewers and other ingredients.

Stir the drained cucumber together with yoghurt, garlic and lemon juice. Season to taste with salt and pepper.

Preheat your barbecue and prepare your skewers. Place a few pieces of meat and veggies on each skewer and drizzle liberally with olive oil, salt and pepper.

Grill the skewers for a few minutes on each side. Serve with Tzatziki Sauce.

Cook's Note

If using wooden skewers, make sure to soak them in water for several hours beforehand so they won't burn.

Given all the beautiful home-grown lamb in New Zealand, I wanted to make a lamb recipe that would do it justice. All the lovely spices used on the lamb pair beautifully with the cool, crunchy raw vegetables in the salad. This one is great for summertime when you can use a barbecue grill, although you could just as easily pan-fry the lamb chops.

MOROCCAN SPICED LAMB CHOPS WITH ROASTED CAULIFLOWER 'COUSCOUS' SALAD

Serves 4

coconut oil, melted, as needed

1 tsp ground cinnamon

1 tsp ground cumin

1 tsp ground coriander

1 tsp chilli powder

1 tsp paprika

1 tsp salt

4 lamb leg chops

Roasted Cauliflower 'Couscous' Salad

1 small head cauliflower

2 tbsp olive oil

salt and pepper to taste

juice of 1 lemon

1 small red onion, diced

1 cucumber, diced

2–3 tomatoes, diced

¼ cup loosely packed fresh parsley, finely chopped

¼ cup loosely packed fresh mint, finely chopped

¾ cup crumbled feta (optional)

To make Roasted Cauliflower 'Couscous' Salad, preheat oven to 200°C. Cut cauliflower into large chunks and run them through the grating attachment of a food processor, or grate by hand.

Spread cauliflower over a baking tray and drizzle with olive oil, salt and pepper, then toss to coat evenly. Roast for 10–12 minutes until cooked and slightly browned. Set aside to cool to room temperature.

Meanwhile, preheat barbecue to a medium-high heat and brush grill with coconut oil. Alternatively, heat a grill pan over a medium-high heat on the stovetop.

Mix cinnamon, cumin, coriander, chilli powder, paprika and salt in a small mixing bowl. Rub the mixture into both sides of the lamb chops.

Grill chops for about 3 minutes per side, depending on thickness (about 3 minutes for medium-thick chops). Allow to rest for 3 minutes.

Place cauliflower in a bowl and stir in lemon juice, red onion, cucumber, tomato, parsley, mint and feta, if using. Serve lamb chops alongside the Roasted Cauliflower 'Couscous' Salad.

The ultimate comfort food! Perhaps not quite like your mum used to make it, but I know you'll still love this delicious primal version of a classic dish.

SHEPHERD'S PIE

Serves 4–6

Topping

1 kg orange kumara

¼ cup cream (or coconut cream for dairy-free)

3 tbsp butter (optional)

salt and pepper to taste

1 egg yolk

¼ cup grated Parmesan (optional)

Filling

2 tbsp olive oil or bacon fat

1 large onion, chopped

2 carrots, peeled and finely diced

2 cloves garlic, finely diced

1 kg minced lamb

2 tsp tomato paste

1 cup Chicken Stock (page 154)

1 tsp dried rosemary

½ tsp chopped fresh thyme

½ cup frozen peas, thawed

Peel kumara and cut into chunks, then place in a pot and cover with cold water. Set over a high heat, cover and bring to a boil. Reduce to a simmer and cook until soft, about 15–20 minutes.

While the kumara is simmering, prepare the filling. Preheat oven to 200°C.

Heat olive oil or bacon fat in a frying-pan over a medium-high heat. Add onion and carrot and sauté until the onion softens, about 3–4 minutes. Stir garlic in and continue cooking for another minute.

Add in minced lamb, breaking it up as it cooks, and cook until browned and almost cooked through. Stir in tomato paste, stock, rosemary and thyme. Bring to a boil, then reduce the heat to low, cover and simmer for about 10–12 minutes or until the sauce has thickened slightly.

Drain the kumara and return to the saucepan. Mash until smooth, then stir in the cream or coconut cream, butter, if using, and salt and pepper. Stir in the yolk last and mix until well combined.

Stir peas into lamb mixture, then pour it into a buttered casserole dish. Spread kumara mash over the top, sprinkle with Parmesan, if using, and bake for 25 minutes or until slightly browned on top.

Sweet Stuff

Naturally sweet desserts and treats

The barbecue isn't just for meat! Grilling is a delicious way to prepare fruit for a fantastic summer dessert. Here's one of my favourite ways to do it . . .

GRILLED PINEAPPLE WITH MASCARPONE AND FRESH BLUEBERRIES

Serves 3–4

100 g mascarpone

½ tsp Vanilla Extract (page 168)

½ ripe pineapple, peeled and sliced into rounds ½ cm thick

6 tbsp melted coconut oil

½ cup fresh blueberries

Whisk mascarpone and vanilla together and set aside.

Light your barbecue and set it to a medium-high heat.

Brush pineapple slices with coconut oil, then grill until browned and slightly caramelised, about 2–3 minutes per side.

Remove pineapple to a platter or serving plates and top each slice with a dollop of vanilla mascarpone and a few blueberries.

I started making this recipe way back in culinary school, when I was still pretty new to primal eating. One instructor in particular told me how much he liked it, not even knowing he was eating a primal dessert. This is why it will always be one of my favourites.

HONEY VANILLA PANNA COTTA WITH FIG COMPOTE

Serves 4

Panna Cotta

3 tbsp cold water

1 tsp powdered gelatine

2 cups cream

⅓ cup honey

1 vanilla pod

½ cup roughly chopped toasted pistachios, to serve

Fig Compote

250 g dried figs, stems removed, roughly chopped

250 g prunes, roughly chopped

zest and juice of 1 orange

1 tsp ground cardamom

1 tsp ground cinnamon

1½ cups water

For the Panna Cotta, place cold water in a bowl, sprinkle gelatine over the top and stir gently. Allow gelatine to soften while you prepare your other ingredients.

Pour 1½ cups of cream into a saucepan with the honey. Split the vanilla pod and scrape the seeds into the cream and honey, then add the entire pod. Heat the mixture slowly over a medium heat, stirring often, until it just begins to simmer.

Remove from heat and stir gelatine into the mixture. It should immediately melt into the cream.

Stir in remaining cream (this will help to bring down the temperature of the mixture faster). Remove the vanilla pod and pour the Panna Cotta mixture into four glasses or ramekins. Refrigerate for at least 4 hours, or overnight, until set.

To make the Fig Compote, combine all the ingredients in a saucepan over a medium heat. Bring to a low simmer and cook, stirring occasionally, for 8–10 minutes until thickened. Cool completely, then store in the refrigerator. It will thicken more as it cools.

Serve Panna Cotta topped with Fig Compote and toasted pistachios.

It's bacon. It's maple syrup. It's dessert. Trust me, you want to try this one. It's a flavour explosion. Just be ready for how incredible your kitchen will smell with these in the oven.

BAKED STUFFED PEARS

Serves 4

2 ripe Anjou pears

¼ cup Creamy Goat's Cheese (page 150)

¼ cup chopped pecans, lightly toasted

1 tbsp pure maple syrup

4 rashers streaky bacon (the good stuff – with no weird preservatives or added sugars!)

Preheat oven to 180°C. Line a baking sheet with non-stick paper.

Slice pears in half lengthwise and scoop out the cores.

In a small bowl, fold goat's cheese, chopped pecans and maple syrup together.

Fill the cavity of each pear with a heaped tablespoon of the cheese mixture, then wrap pear with a rasher of bacon. (Don't let the bacon overlap too much or it won't get crispy.)

Lay the pears on the baking sheet and bake for about 25–30 minutes, or until the pears are soft and the bacon is crispy.

This is a great dish to make in the summertime, when you can visit local farms and pick your own berries. I have a personal favourite spot for getting fresh blueberries close to home – you can't beat fresh and local!

CHOCOLATE CRÈME CHANTILLY WITH FRESH BERRIES

Serves 4

90 g dark chocolate (at least 70% cocoa solids), finely chopped

1½ cups cream (or coconut cream for dairy-free)

1½ cups fresh berries

Place chocolate in a medium-sized bowl.

Heat cream in a small saucepan over a moderate heat until just simmering, watching it carefully so it does not boil over.

Immediately pour hot cream over chocolate and allow to sit for 30 seconds before stirring. Whisk the mixture well, until chocolate and cream are fully combined.

Cover and place in refrigerator until completely chilled, 3–4 hours. If you try to whip it while it's still warm, you will be whipping for a very long time!

Once fully chilled, use electric beaters (or a strong arm and a whisk) to whip the cream until it forms soft peaks.

Serve with fresh berries, or just a spoon.

Cook's Note

Be sure to watch your cream closely when heating it – cream will go from motionless to boiled-over mess in the blink of an eye. I know. I've done it a hundred times.

This recipe was inspired by one of my best friends, the brilliant and beautiful chocolatier Agnes Almeida. I hope I made her proud with this one.

BITTERSWEET HOT CHOCOLATE WITH A KICK

Serves 2

- 2 cups coconut milk
- ½ tsp Vanilla Extract (page 168)
- ½ tsp chilli powder
- ½ tsp ground cinnamon
- pinch of salt
- 120 g dark chocolate (at least 70% cocoa solids), finely chopped
- 1 recipe Whipped Coconut Cream (page 168), made ahead

Combine coconut milk, vanilla, chilli powder, cinnamon and salt in a saucepan over a medium heat. Bring just to a simmer, then remove from the heat (watch it carefully so it does not boil over!).

Immediately add chopped chocolate to the pan and wait 30 seconds for the chocolate to begin to melt. Then use a stick blender to emulsify the chocolate and coconut milk mixture until well blended.

Serve hot with a dollop of Whipped Coconut Cream.

Cook's Note

You need to remember to put the coconut cream in the refrigerator the day before serving.

This is like American pumpkin pie, without the crust! Delicious, rich and filling as this is, the crust is totally unnecessary. Orange Kumara Purée is a baking essential in a true Primal Kitchen; it has so many uses!

BAKED SWEET KUMARA CUSTARD

Serves 6

- 1½ cups full-fat coconut milk
- ¼ cup liquid honey or pure maple syrup
- 4 egg yolks
- 1 cup Orange Kumara Purée (page 149)
- 1 tsp Vanilla Extract (page 168)
- 1 tsp ground cinnamon
- ½ tsp freshly grated nutmeg
- pinch of salt

Preheat oven to 170°C.

Whisk together coconut milk, honey or maple syrup, egg yolks, kumara purée, vanilla, cinnamon, nutmeg and salt until thoroughly combined.

Divide the mixture evenly among six ramekins and place on a baking sheet.

Place the baking sheet in the oven and bake for 25–30 minutes or until the custards are nearly set but still jiggle slightly in the centre.

Remove from oven and cool ramekins on a wire rack.

A beautiful dessert that is sure to impress your friends, made with the natural sweetness of fresh raspberries.

DARK CHOCOLATE RASPBERRY SOUFFLÉS

Serves 4

½ cup raspberries, plus extra for serving

100 g dark chocolate (at least 70% cocoa solids)

2 tbsp butter (or coconut oil for dairy-free)

4 egg whites

3 egg yolks

Preheat oven to 200°C. Grease four individual ramekins with butter or coconut oil, and set aside.

Purée the ½ cup of raspberries until smooth, then strain the purée through a sieve.

Melt chocolate and butter or coconut oil together in a double boiler or a heatproof bowl set over a pot of simmering water, stirring to combine. Remove from the heat and whisk in the raspberry purée.

In a large bowl, whip the egg whites until they form soft peaks.

Add egg yolks to the cooled chocolate mixture, stirring until smooth and fully combined.

A third at a time, gently fold the whipped egg whites into the chocolate mixture, being careful not to deflate the whites too much.

Pour batter into the prepared ramekins and bake for about 10 minutes, until risen but still slightly jiggly in the centre. Serve immediately, topped with extra raspberries.

Is it a brownie? Is it a cookie? It's actually halfway between the two – a cookie slice! Another great use for our good friend the orange kumara, these bars are one of my favourites.

PRIMAL CHOCOLATE CHIP COOKIE BARS

Makes 16

- 125 g butter, at room temperature
- ¾ cup Date Paste (page 164)
- ¾ cup Orange Kumara Purée (page 149)
- 1 tsp Vanilla Extract (page 168)
- 1 egg
- 1 cup coconut flour
- 1 cup almond flour
- 1 tsp baking soda
- 1 tsp ground cinnamon
- ¼ tsp salt
- 1 cup chopped dark chocolate or dark chocolate chips (at least 70% cocoa solids)

Preheat oven to 170°C. Lightly grease a 20 cm x 20 cm slice tin.

Using an electric mixer, cream butter, Date Paste and Orange Kumara Purée together until smooth. Add vanilla and egg and beat again until combined, scraping down the sides of the bowl as you go.

In a separate bowl, mix coconut flour, almond flour, baking soda, cinnamon and salt together. Add to the kumara mixture and beat until combined. Stir in the chocolate last.

Spread the cookie batter into the baking tin and bake for 30–40 minutes, or until a toothpick stuck into the middle comes out clean.

Cool completely in the pan, then slice and serve!

Semifreddo is an Italian word meaning 'half frozen'. It's sort of like ice cream that you slice. The combination of sweet berries, rich chocolate and bitter coffee in this recipe makes a delicious frozen dessert.

MOCHA BOYSENBERRY SEMIFREDDO

Serves 6

250 g boysenberries, plus extra to serve

3 eggs, separated

100 ml cream

⅓ cup liquid honey

1 shot of coffee (or 1 tsp instant espresso, dissolved according to packet instructions)

50 g dark chocolate (at least 70% cocoa solids), shaved or grated, plus extra to serve

Place boysenberries in a saucepan over a medium heat and cook gently for 2–3 minutes to soften. Set aside to cool completely. Meanwhile, line a small loaf tin with plastic wrap, leaving extra on the sides to wrap around the top later.

Place cooled berries in a blender or food processor, process until smooth, then pass the berry purée through a sieve.

Set up three large bowls – in one put your egg whites, in one (the largest) your yolks and in one your cream.

Whip the egg whites until they just form firm peaks. In the second bowl, whip the yolks with the honey until thick and creamy. Last, whip the cream until it forms medium peaks, whisking in the coffee at the end.

Gently fold the berry purée into the yolks. Next, fold in the whipped egg whites. Last, fold in the cream and the chocolate shavings, being careful not to deflate all the beautiful whipping you just did!

Pour the mixture into the prepared loaf tin, cover the top with the plastic wrap and freeze overnight (or for at least 4–6 hours).

Remove from the freezer 20 minutes before serving. Unmould from the loaf tin and cut into slices. Serve with extra chocolate shavings and boysenberries.

Cook's Note

Pregnant women are recommended to avoid eating raw egg.

Baker's Secret

I think I could write a whole book on orange kumara recipes . . . maybe I will. This creamy, delicious primal dessert is fun to make and to share with friends. The spices give it a gingerbread-like flavour, combined with the goodness of orange kumara! If you've never tried making your own ice cream, I highly recommend it.

SWEET KUMARA ICE CREAM

Serves 4–6

5 egg yolks

1 cup Orange Kumara Purée (page 149)

1 tsp Vanilla Extract (page 168)

2 cups cream (or coconut cream for dairy-free)

½ cup liquid honey (can substitute with Date Paste (page 164) or pure maple syrup)

½ tsp ground cinnamon

½ tsp ground ginger

¼ tsp ground nutmeg

¼ tsp salt

Lightly whisk the egg yolks in a small bowl and set aside.

Whisk kumara purée, vanilla, cream, honey, cinnamon, ginger, nutmeg and salt together in a small saucepan and place over a medium-high heat. Warm the mixture until just barely simmering, then temper in the egg yolks. To do this, ladle one spoonful at a time of the hot cream mixture into the egg yolks, while stirring, to slowly bring the temperature of the yolks up without scrambling them. Once the yolk mixture is warm, pour it back into the saucepan with the rest of the cream mixture and continue heating, stirring constantly, until the mixture has thickened. Do not let it boil.

Remove from the heat once thickened. Chill the mixture for several hours, or overnight. To cool it faster, place the mixture in a metal bowl, set this over a larger bowl filled with ice, and stir slowly to cool it.

Once the custard is well chilled, you may churn it through an ice-cream maker according to its directions. If you don't have an ice-cream maker, you can slow-churn it using a hand mixer. To do this, place the custard in the freezer for a few hours, without freezing it completely. Remove it from the freezer and whip it with a hand mixer for a few minutes to 'churn' some air into it. Return it to the freezer for another 2 hours or so, then whip it once more with the hand mixer and place it back in the freezer to finish freezing. It's a bit more time-consuming, but whipping the air into it gradually will ensure a light, creamy ice cream!

These are a bit labour-intensive – but worth the work, and fun to make anyway! If you have kids, they'll love getting involved in making them.

COCONUT CUPS

Makes about 20

Cups

250 g dark chocolate (at least 70% cocoa solids)

3 tbsp coconut oil

20 mini cupcake wrappers

Coconut Filling

¼ cup coconut threads

¼ cup coconut flour

2 tbsp melted coconut oil

1 tbsp liquid honey

To make the cups, melt chocolate and coconut oil together in a double boiler (or a heatproof bowl set over a pot of gently simmering water), then remove from the heat. Keep the bowl on top of the pot to help keep it warm while you work.

Use a pastry brush or clean small paintbrush to paint a thin layer of chocolate on the insides of the cupcake wrappers. Place them on a baking sheet and then in the freezer to set while you prepare the filling (it won't take long).

For the filling, combine the coconut threads, coconut flour, melted coconut oil and honey in a bowl and stir well to combine.

Fill the hardened chocolate cups nearly to the top with filling, then pour a bit more melted chocolate over the top, just to the edges, to seal everything in. Place the cups back in the freezer for 15 minutes to finish setting. Then share with a primal chocolate-loving friend!

Store Coconut Cups in the refrigerator.

Cook's Note

Other filling options are:

- Banana Almond – ½ very ripe banana, ½ cup almond flour, 2 teaspoons of honey and a pinch of salt, mashed together until smooth
- Homemade Nut Butter – see recipe page 164
- Triple-berry Chia – 1 cup thawed frozen mixed berries and 2 teaspoons of chia seeds: blend the berries until smooth, stir chia seeds in and refrigerate for at least 1 hour, until thickened.

Macadamias are hands down my favourite nut. I'll look for any excuse to buy them. They add a great texture to this sweet yet tart parfait and look beautiful dished up. You need to start making the Whipped Coconut Cream for this recipe the day before serving, and it's best to make the Grapefruit Curd ahead of time, too.

COCONUT AND FRUIT PARFAIT WITH MACADAMIA CRUMBLE

Serves 4

1 recipe Grapefruit Curd (page 166), made ahead

1 recipe Whipped Coconut Cream (page 168), made ahead

1 grapefruit, peeled and segmented

1 cup fresh strawberries, sliced

Crumble

¾ cup raw, shelled macadamia nuts, roughly chopped

¾ cup coconut threads

pinch of salt

1 tbsp melted coconut oil

Combine all crumble ingredients in a pan over a medium heat. Cook, stirring often, just until the nuts and coconut are golden and toasted. This will only take a few minutes – watch them carefully so they don't burn! Remove from the heat and set aside to cool completely.

To assemble the parfait, layer Grapefruit Curd, Whipped Coconut Cream, crumble, grapefruit segments and sliced strawberries among four clear glasses or Mason jars. Serve up and share with friends!

Granny Smith apples are so sweet yet tart, you don't need to add any other sweeteners to this filling to make it delicious. Great with fresh whipped cream.

BAKED NUTTY APPLE CRUMBLE

Serves 4–6

Filling

3–4 Granny Smith apples, peeled and cut into chunks

2 tsp ground cinnamon

1 tsp ground nutmeg

1 tsp ground ginger

¼ tsp flaky salt

1 tsp almond extract (see Cook's Note on page 168)

3 tbsp melted butter

whipped cream or Whipped Coconut Cream (page 168), to serve

Crumble Topping

½ cup chopped pecans

¼ cup chopped walnuts

¼ cup almond flour

2 tsp ground cinnamon

1½ tbsp melted butter or coconut oil

3 tbsp liquid honey

Preheat oven to 180°C.

Combine apples, cinnamon, nutmeg, ginger, salt, almond extract and melted butter, and stir to coat the apples evenly. Spread the mixture into a baking dish.

Stir together all of the crumble ingredients and sprinkle on top of the apples.

Bake for about 30–40 minutes until the top is golden brown and the apples are tender but still crisp.

Serve warm with fresh whipped cream or Whipped Coconut Cream.

Cook's Note

If using Whipped Coconut Cream you need to remember to put the coconut cream in the refrigerator the day before serving.

My partner once ate an entire tray of these in one sitting. I don't recommend this, but he can tell you how hard they were to resist for afternoon tea.

EARL GREY SHORTBREAD

Makes about 12

- 1 cup coconut flour
- ¼ cup tapioca flour
- 2 bags Earl Grey tea leaves (approx. 1 tbsp loose leaves)
- pinch of salt
- ½ cup melted butter or coconut oil
- 2 egg yolks
- ¼ cup liquid honey
- 1 tsp Vanilla Extract (page 168)

Preheat oven to 170°C. Lightly grease a baking sheet, or line with non-stick paper.

Mix coconut flour, tapioca flour, tea leaves and salt together in a large bowl.

In a separate bowl, combine melted butter or coconut oil, egg yolks, honey and vanilla.

Combine all of the ingredients, stirring until it forms a solid dough (it will be slightly crumbly).

Using a rolling pin, roll out the cookie dough on a cutting board or worktop to a thickness of about 1 cm. Cut into squares (or any shape you like!), place on the baking sheet and bake for 8–10 minutes until golden brown. Cool on a wire rack.

Cook's Note

For a Chai Spice version, omit the tea leaves and instead use 1 teaspoon of ground cinnamon, 1 teaspoon of ground cardamom, 1 teaspoon of ground ginger and ½ teaspoon of ground nutmeg.

When I was a teenager, I baked America's famous Nestlé Toll House Chocolate Chip Cookies recipe about a million times. That recipe is imprinted in my brain forever. When I started doing primal baking, I knew I had to come up with the perfect primal cookie recipe to match those Nestlé cookies I always used to make. This is it!

CHOCOLATE CHIP AND WALNUT COOKIES

Makes 14

125 g butter, softened
½ cup Date Paste (page 164)
1 egg
1 tsp Vanilla Extract (page 168)
½ cup almond flour
½ cup coconut flour
1 tsp ground cinnamon
½ tsp baking soda
¼ tsp salt
¼ cup dark chocolate chips (at least 70% cocoa solids)
¼ cup chopped walnuts

Preheat oven to 170°C. Lightly grease a baking sheet, or line with non-stick paper.

Using a stand mixer or hand-held beaters, beat softened butter and Date Paste together until smooth and creamy.

Mix in egg and vanilla and continue beating until incorporated.

Stir in almond flour, coconut flour, cinnamon, baking soda and salt, and beat until combined.

Stir in dark chocolate chips and chopped walnuts.

Drop spoonfuls of the cookie dough a few centimetres apart on the baking sheet. Use the back of the spoon to flatten the cookies down slightly.

Bake for 12–15 minutes until golden, then allow to cool completely on the baking sheet.

This recipe was inspired by Julia Child's chocolate mousse, found in a book given to me by my grandmother. This stuff is incredible, and you'd never guess it came out of a 'healthy cookbook'. You could easily serve this to friends, then watch their jaws drop when you tell them it's primal! I think even Julia Child might have approved . . .

CHOCOLATE MOCHA MOUSSE

Serves 4

250 g dark chocolate (at least 70% cocoa solids)

4 eggs, separated

2 tbsp cold coffee

2 tsp powdered gelatine

50 g unsalted butter, cut into small pieces, at room temperature

Begin by melting chocolate in a double boiler or in a heatproof bowl set over a pot of simmering water. Meanwhile, whip egg whites in a large bowl until they form stiff peaks.

Pour cold coffee into a small microwave-safe bowl, sprinkle gelatine over and allow to sit for a few minutes to soften. Then microwave on high for just a few seconds (4 or 5) to completely dissolve the gelatine.

Remove the top part of the double boiler or the bowl from the heat, and whisk gelatine into the melted chocolate. Add egg yolks while whisking, and continue to whisk until smooth. Stir in the butter last. (The mixture will be quite thick and will look funny at first before coming together. Just keep mixing!)

Gently fold in a third of the whipped egg whites at a time, until totally incorporated.

Pour the mousse into four serving glasses, cover with plastic wrap and refrigerate for at least 3 hours, or overnight.

Cook's Note

Pregnant women are recommended to avoid eating raw egg.

I love using kumara in desserts – it's featured in a lot of my sweet recipes. Orange kumara is so naturally sweet, and adds great texture to many different dishes. I always keep a container of puréed kumara on hand in my freezer.

KUMARA GINGER CRUMBLE SLICE

Makes 12 slices

Base

1½ cups almond flour
½ cup tapioca flour
1 tsp baking powder
1 tsp baking soda
1 tbsp ground ginger
2 tsp ground cinnamon
½ tsp ground nutmeg
½ tsp salt
½ cup Orange Kumara Purée (page 149)
½ cup melted coconut oil
½ cup blackstrap molasses
1 egg
1 tsp Vanilla Extract (page 168)

Crumble Topping

½ cup sliced almonds
½ cup coconut threads
½ cup almond flour
2 tsp ground cinnamon
1 tsp ground ginger
3 tbsp melted butter or coconut oil
3 tbsp honey

Preheat oven to 170°C. Lightly grease a 20 cm x 20 cm slice tin.

Mix together almond flour, tapioca flour, baking powder, baking soda, ginger, cinnamon, nutmeg and salt in a bowl until well combined.

In a separate large bowl, whisk kumara, coconut oil, molasses, egg and vanilla together. Stir in the flour mixture and mix well to combine. Spread the slice batter into the tin.

Stir together all the ingredients for the topping and sprinkle over the top of the slice.

Bake for about 25–30 minutes, or until golden and cooked through. Cool completely in the tin before slicing.

These are delicious served with fresh whipped cream or yoghurt.

The combination of strawberries and rhubarb reminds me of my grandmother. She always made strawberry rhubarb pies in the summer when I visited her as a kid. The sweetness of the strawberries together with the tartness of the rhubarb is perfection. This cake is for her!

STRAWBERRY RHUBARB CRUMBLE CAKE

Serves 6–8

Crumble Topping

½ cup tapioca flour

¼ cup almond flour

½ cup coconut threads

½ cup Date Paste (page 164)

40 g cold butter, cut into 1 cm cubes

Cake

1 cup coconut flour

½ cup almond flour

1½ tsp baking powder

1 tsp baking soda

125 g butter, at room temperature

¾ cup Date Paste (page 164)

1 tsp Vanilla Extract (page 168)

3 eggs

1 cup chopped strawberries, 2 cm pieces

1 cup chopped rhubarb, 2 cm pieces

Preheat oven to 170°C. Lightly grease a 20 cm round cake tin.

To make the topping, stir together tapioca flour, almond flour and coconut threads in a small bowl. Using a fork (or your hands), mash the Date Paste and cold butter into the flour mixture to form a coarse crumble. Set aside.

For the cake, mix together coconut flour, almond flour, baking powder and baking soda.

Separately, using a stand mixer or hand-held beaters, cream the butter and second measure of Date Paste together until smooth and well combined.

Beat in vanilla and eggs, one egg at a time, until fully incorporated. Add the flour mixture and continue mixing until just combined.

Spread half of the cake batter into the cake tin (it will be very thick). Scatter half of the strawberry and rhubarb pieces over the top of the batter. Spread the remaining batter over the fruit, followed by the rest of the strawberry and rhubarb. Sprinkle the top with the crumble mixture, pressing down lightly, and bake for 40–45 minutes until golden brown on top.

Cool completely in cake tin before serving.

Primal Basics

Super-charged sauces, dressings and sides

Cauliflower rice is such a fun side dish to make. It's delicious and looks so much like real rice, you'll find you really don't miss the other stuff!

BASIC CAULIFLOWER RICE

Serves 4

1 small cauliflower
1 tbsp olive oil
salt and pepper to taste

Cut cauliflower into large chunks and pass through the grater attachment of a food processor, or grate by hand. Use large-sized grater holes.

Heat olive oil in a large pan over a medium heat. Once hot, stir in cauliflower and cook, stirring occasionally, until slightly browned and cooked through. Season to taste with salt and pepper.

These hearty little dinner rolls are great served warm with a smear of butter, and even better with roasted bone marrow from Braised Beef Shins (page 93).

PRIMAL DINNER ROLLS

Makes 5–6

¼ cup ground linseed
½ cup coconut flour
¾ tsp baking soda
½ tsp salt
cayenne pepper to taste
1 egg
4 egg whites
¼ cup olive oil

Preheat oven to 170°C. Lightly grease a baking sheet, or line with non-stick paper.

Combine ground linseed, coconut flour, baking soda, salt and cayenne pepper in a large mixing bowl.

In a separate bowl, whisk egg, egg whites and olive oil together.

Whisk the egg mixture into the dry ingredients. As you whisk, the coconut flour will begin to absorb a lot of the moisture and the batter will get very thick.

Drop large spoonfuls of batter onto the baking sheet and bake for about 20–25 minutes, until cooked through and browned slightly on top.

Serve warm.

These 'tortillas' are more like super-versatile crêpes. They can be used for savoury or sweet dishes, hot or cold!

PRIMAL TORTILLAS

Makes about 8–9 medium-sized tortillas

½ cup tapioca flour
¼ cup ground linseed
5 egg whites
2 tbsp cider vinegar
1 tsp baking powder
50 g melted butter
1 cup coconut milk
¼ tsp salt
1 tbsp coconut oil for cooking

Whisk together all ingredients except coconut oil, until very well combined. It will be quite runny.

Heat coconut oil in a pancake pan over a medium-high heat. Once hot, pour about ¼ cup of batter into the pan, tilting it around to spread a thin, even layer across the surface.

Cook for 1–2 minutes on one side, then flip and cook for another minute on the other side. Continue until all the batter is cooked. Stack cooked tortillas on a plate with layers of baking paper or greaseproof paper in between to help stop them sticking together. If serving right away, use a warmed plate and cover with a clean tea towel.

Use immediately, or store in an airtight container in the refrigerator for up to a week.

Cook's Note

Save the yolks from your eggs for making Paleo Aïoli (page 155) or Sweet Kumara Ice Cream (page 127).

Orange kumara is probably my favourite vegetable on Earth. If I could, I'd eat it with everything. (In fact, I often do.) This is a great snack or side dish.

BAKED KUMARA WEDGES

Serves 4

2 eggs
3 tbsp full-fat milk
½ cup almond flour
⅓ cup coconut flour
¼ cup finely grated Parmesan
1 tsp salt
¼ tsp garlic powder
¼ tsp black pepper
pinch of cayenne pepper
1 kg orange kumara, cut into wedges

Preheat oven to 180°C. Lightly grease a baking sheet, or line with non-stick paper.

Whisk eggs and milk together in a dish.

Separately, combine almond flour, coconut flour, Parmesan, salt, garlic powder, black pepper and cayenne pepper in a shallow bowl.

Dredge kumara wedges first in the egg mixture and then in the 'breading' mixture, coating well, before placing them on the baking sheet. Bake until golden and cooked through, about 25–35 minutes (it depends on how thick you cut them).

You can choose whether to peel the kumara or not before you cook it – some like it peeled, others wouldn't do without it. This is delicious either way.

GOLDEN KUMARA MASH

Serves 4

4 medium-sized golden kumara, cut into chunks
2 tbsp butter
¼ cup cream or coconut cream
salt and pepper to taste

Place kumara chunks in a large pot and cover with water. Bring to a boil, then reduce to a simmer and continue cooking until kumara are soft and cooked through, about 20 minutes.

Drain kumara well, then return them to their cooking pot and mash with a potato masher. Add in butter and cream or coconut cream and continue to mash to mix in. Season to taste with salt and pepper.

Cauliflower purée is a great alternative to mashed potatoes when 'primalising' your favourite meals. And cauliflower is lower in carbohydrate and more nutritious than plain white potatoes – bonus!

SIMPLE CAULIFLOWER PURÉE

Serves 4

1 small cauliflower (or ½ a large one)
2 tbsp olive oil
salt and pepper to taste
1 tbsp butter
½–¾ cup full-fat milk or coconut milk

Preheat oven to 180°C.

Cut cauliflower into small chunks and place in a roasting dish. Toss with olive oil and season with salt and pepper. Roast for 25–30 minutes, until cooked through. Remove from oven and allow to cool slightly.

Place cauliflower in a food processor and process until fine. Add in butter and milk or coconut milk a little at a time, with the blade running, until you get a smooth, creamy texture. You may not need to use all of it. Season to taste with more salt and pepper. Serve warm.

When I lived in the US, canned pumpkin purée was a staple in my pantry. I was gutted when I moved to New Zealand and couldn't find it anywhere! But sweet orange kumara is a perfect alternative.

ORANGE KUMARA PURÉE

Makes 3–4 cups, depending on the size of the kumara

2–3 large orange kumara

Peel and chop the kumara, and place in a large pot of water. Bring to a boil and simmer for 15–20 minutes, until soft. Drain, then allow to cool slightly.

Purée the kumara in a food processor or with a stick blender until very smooth.

Use straight away in your favourite primal dishes, or freeze in cup-sized amounts for a later date.

I'm obsessed with goat's cheese. It's delicious either sweet or savoury, and surprisingly easy to make yourself. I use cider vinegar for its mild flavour, but you could use any acid to curdle the milk – lemon juice or any other acidic cooking agents you have in your pantry. Play with it and see what you like best!

CREAMY GOAT'S CHEESE

Makes about 1 cup

- large square of cheesecloth
- 1 litre goat's milk
- cooking thermometer
- 1½ tbsp cider vinegar

Line a large sieve with the cheesecloth, place it over a large bowl and set aside.

In a small saucepan over a medium heat, heat the goat's milk. You want to heat it slowly – if you turn your back on it for a minute, it can boil over and make a giant mess. I know because I've done it! Set the thermometer in the pot with the milk and watch it carefully.

Once the milk reaches 80°C, remove it from the heat and immediately add the vinegar, without stirring. Let it sit for a minute. Then, gently begin to stir the milk – you should see curdles beginning to form. It'll only take a few minutes.

Slowly pour the curdled milk into the lined sieve, and tie up the cheesecloth at the top. Leave it in your refrigerator for a few hours (or preferably overnight) to drain, and you'll have creamy, delicious goat's cheese! You can also pour the whey in the bowl off and store it in the refrigerator for a few days, to use in other recipes. It's good used in soups in place of some or all of the stock.

Once you've made your cheese, you can have fun with flavouring it any way you like. I'll add a bit of sea salt and some fresh herbs. Or, to make it sweet, fold in a bit of cinnamon and honey. It will keep in the refrigerator for a few days, but is best used fresh.

Cook's Note

If goat products aren't your thing, you can do the same process with full-fat cow's milk, and you've got ricotta cheese!

I love making my own fermented veggies, especially beetroot. The healthy bacteria in fermented vegetables helps keep your gut healthy and makes a tasty addition to any meal.

FERMENTED BEETROOT

Makes 1 large jar

- 3 cups water
- 1 tbsp sea salt
- 3–4 medium-sized beetroots
- 3–4 cloves garlic, crushed
- 1 tsp black peppercorns
- 1 tbsp whey

Combine water and sea salt in a small pot over a high heat, and bring to a simmer. Cook for just long enough to dissolve the salt, then remove from the heat. Allow to cool to room temperature.

Slice beetroot into very thin rounds, as thin as you can make them. If you have a mandoline slicer, this would be a great time to get it out.

Place crushed garlic, peppercorns and whey in a glass jar, followed by the beetroot. Layer the beetroot as closely as possible to fit it all in. Pour the cooled salt water into the jar until it almost reaches the top and all of the beetroot is submerged. Cover with the lid and set aside on a table or pantry shelf.

Once or twice a day, unscrew the lid of the jar to release any air. The lovely live bacteria growing in the jar will create gas – if you forget to release the air, it may bubble over (I know from experience . . .).

After three days at room temperature, the beetroot should begin to take on a delicious pickle-like scent. At this point you can transfer the fermented beetroot to the refrigerator. The bacteria won't die at refrigerator temperatures, but its rate of growth will slow to an almost hibernation-like state. The beetroot is best eaten after at least two weeks in the refrigerator, after the flavours have developed.

Cook's Note

You can acquire whey by buying plain probiotic yoghurt (check the label). The clear liquid that forms on the top of the yoghurt in its container – that's whey!

Homemade chicken stock might sound a little scary, but it's not as hard as you might think. Stock is the base for so many healthy dishes, and making it yourself is really satisfying. It's much better for you than the store-bought stuff, which usually contains excess salt or sugar, and preservatives.

CHICKEN STOCK

Makes about 2½ litres

1 kg chicken frames

3 cloves garlic, crushed

3 celery stalks, roughly chopped

2 medium onions, roughly chopped

2 large carrots, roughly chopped

2 bay leaves

small bunch of fresh parsley

2–3 sprigs fresh thyme

1 tbsp black peppercorns

3 litres cold water

Place chicken frames, garlic, vegetables, herbs and peppercorns in a large stockpot. Add cold water and bring to a boil, then reduce to a simmer.

Keep the stock at a low simmer for 3–4 hours, occasionally skimming the residue off the top of the liquid with a spoon.

Strain the stock through a fine sieve, and store in your refrigerator or freezer.

Cook's Note

You can find chicken frames in the meat section of any grocery store. If there are none on display, ask the meat department for some and they will be happy to package some up for you. They usually come with a good bit of meat still on the bones.

Making homemade aïoli is a bit intimidating for some people, but it's really much easier than you think. Just take your time with it. You'll never regret pouring your oil into the mixture too slowly, but you'll know if you've done it too fast!

PALEO AÏOLI (PALEOLI!)

Makes about 1¾ cups

2 egg yolks
1½ tbsp lemon juice
1½ cups olive oil or avocado oil
1 clove garlic, finely diced
1 tsp ground black pepper
salt to taste

Manual version – place egg yolks and lemon juice in a large bowl and immediately start whisking. (If you leave the lemon juice and yolks together too long without stirring, the acid in the lemon juice will start to 'cook' your yolks!)

Begin by pouring a teaspoon of oil at a time into the yolk mixture, while whisking, until incorporated. Continue whisking and drizzling the oil into the bowl simultaneously. It will begin to thicken and become pale in colour.

Continue until all of the oil has been used. At this point you should have a beautiful, thick, creamy texture! If it is too thick, whisk in a tablespoon or so of warm water to thin the mixture a bit. Whisk in the garlic, pepper and salt.

Blender version – place egg yolks and lemon juice in a blender or food processor and turn it on. With the machine running, slowly drizzle oil in, a little at a time, until all of the oil is incorporated. Add in the garlic, pepper and salt.

Store aïoli in an airtight container in the refrigerator.

Cook's Note

Pouring your oil into a measuring cup or other lipped cup before starting will make it easier to drizzle into your aïoli.

I prefer avocado oil in this recipe for its mild flavour.

Tomato sauce is another classic accompaniment that is likely to be loaded with sugar and preservatives if you buy it ready-made. Not to worry, though – making it at home is a cinch, and actually less expensive than buying the jarred stuff!

PRIMAL TOMATO SAUCE

Makes about 3 cups

2 tbsp olive oil
1 onion, diced
1 carrot, peeled and grated
3 cloves garlic, finely diced
1 tsp dried oregano
1 tsp dried thyme
1 tsp dried basil
1 bay leaf
2 cans diced tomatoes (800 g total)
1 tbsp honey

Heat olive oil in a saucepan over a medium heat. Add onion and carrot and cook, stirring occasionally, for 3–4 minutes until they begin to soften. Stir in garlic and continue cooking for another minute.

Add oregano, thyme, basil, bay leaf, tomatoes and honey. Bring the sauce to a simmer and cook, stirring occasionally, for 15 minutes, then remove from the heat.

Allow the sauce to cool slightly, then remove the bay leaf and blend the sauce with a stick blender or food processor until smooth.

Store in an airtight container in the refrigerator.

Here's another great condiment to serve with your favourite primal dishes. Rather than cooking it with several cups of sugar, like most barbecue sauces, this one uses the natural sweetness of berries and tart green apple to give it its flavour.

SWEET AND SMOKY BOYSENBERRY BARBECUE SAUCE

Makes about 3 cups

- 2 tbsp bacon fat (or other healthy cooking fat or oil)
- 2 small onions, chopped
- 2 cloves garlic, finely diced
- 1 tbsp ground ginger
- 1 tbsp smoked paprika
- 1 tsp cayenne pepper
- 2 cups frozen boysenberries, thawed (including juices)
- 1 tart green apple, peeled and chopped
- 1 can (400 g) chopped tomatoes in juice
- ¼ cup blackstrap molasses
- salt and pepper to taste

Heat fat in a saucepan over a medium heat and add onion. Cook for a few minutes until soft, then add garlic, ginger, smoked paprika and cayenne pepper, and cook for another minute.

Stir in boysenberries, apple, tomatoes and molasses and bring to a boil, then reduce to a low simmer. Allow to cook for about 15 minutes, then remove from the heat and cool slightly.

Purée the mixture using a stick blender or food processor until very smooth, then strain the barbecue sauce through a sieve. Season to taste with salt and pepper.

Store in an airtight container in the refrigerator.

Cook's Note

You can adjust the amount of cayenne pepper in this recipe to make it as spicy or as mild as you like. As it is, it's fairly mild.

I think I've made this guacamole for every football party I've ever been to. It's the ultimate dip! I love it with carrot sticks, capsicum wedges or raw cauliflower florets. The secret is out . . .

SARAH'S TOP-SECRET GUACAMOLE

Serves 4–6 as a side dish

- 3–4 ripe avocados
- juice of 1 lime
- 4 cloves garlic, finely diced
- 3–4 chipotle peppers, finely diced
- 2 ripe vine tomatoes, diced
- 1 red onion, diced
- small handful of fresh coriander, chopped
- salt and pepper to taste

Mash up the avocados in a bowl, leaving some chunkiness. Stir in lime juice, garlic and chipotle peppers, then gently stir in tomatoes, onion and coriander.

Season to taste with salt and pepper. Here you may add more chipotle if, like me, you like your guac pretty spicy. (For less spiciness, scrape the seeds out of the peppers before adding to the guacamole.)

Cook's Note

You can find tinned chipotle peppers in Adobo sauce at the grocery store. Be sure to use a brand that has no added sugar!

Making salad dressing in a jar is a convenient, easy way to do it. Shake it all up to mix it together, then it's already in a container you can store in your fridge.

CITRUS VINAIGRETTE

Makes 12 servings

¼ cup white wine vinegar
¼ cup freshly squeezed orange juice
¼ cup fresh lemon juice
¾ cup olive oil
salt and pepper to taste

Place all ingredients in a jar, close the lid, shake it up – and you're done!

Sesame paste has a beautiful, nutty taste that adds great flavour to salads, while being nut-free for those with allergies. This lovely creamy dressing pairs well with any combination of meat and veggies.

TAHINI DRESSING

Makes 12 servings

½ cup lemon juice
½ cup extra virgin olive oil
⅓ cup tahini (sesame paste)
2 cloves garlic, finely diced
salt and pepper to taste

Place everything in a blender or food processor and process until smooth.

Balsamic vinaigrette is a classic salad dressing. Using a good-quality balsamic vinegar will add a tangy richness to your meal.

BALSAMIC VINAIGRETTE

Makes 12 servings

¾ cup balsamic vinegar
¾ cup extra virgin olive oil
3 tbsp wholegrain mustard
salt and pepper to taste

Place all ingredients in a jar, close the lid, and shake it up. Boom! Salad dressing.

This dressing is really full of spring flavours. The fresh herbs and creamy avocado blend together to make it a gorgeous shade of green that looks as good as it tastes.

GREEN GODDESS DRESSING

Makes 12 servings

1 cup crème fraîche or sour cream
1 avocado
1 spring onion, roughly chopped
1 tsp dried tarragon
1 tsp dried parsley
1 tbsp white wine vinegar
1 clove garlic, coarsely chopped
salt and pepper to taste

Place everything in a blender or food processor and process until smooth.

I like to experiment with different combinations of nuts and herbs when making my own pesto. Classic pesto is made with basil and pine nuts, but you can try any fresh herbs and nuts that you like. This is one of my favourite ways to make it.

FRESH HERB PESTO

Makes about 1 cup

¼ cup walnuts, toasted

3 cloves garlic, finely diced

½ cup grated Parmesan

1 cup loosely packed fresh basil leaves

1 cup loosely packed fresh rocket

½ cup extra virgin olive oil

salt to taste

Place walnuts, garlic and Parmesan in a food processor and pulse to combine and chop the nuts.

Add basil and rocket, and pulse until everything comes together. With the food processor running, slowly drizzle in the oil to combine. You may use more or less oil to reach the desired consistency – the pesto should be smooth and creamy. Season with salt to taste.

Nut butters are easy to make – all you need is a decent food processor.

ALMOND BUTTER

Makes about 1 cup

2 cups almonds
sea salt to taste

Preheat oven to 180°C.

Place almonds on a baking tray. Bake for about 7–8 minutes, stir, then continue baking for another 5 minutes or so. They can burn pretty easily, so keep an eye on them; you want them just toasted.

Allow the nuts to cool, then place in a food processor. Start processing them on a low setting; then, as the nuts get chopped up, increase the speed to high. It will take several minutes, but you will see the mixture turn from finely ground nuts to a chunky paste, then finally to a smooth butter. Add sea salt to taste.

Cook's Note

You can do the same process with any kind of tree nut, or even combine them with toasted sunflower seeds to make sunflower butter. If you use hazelnuts, be sure to remove their skins before putting them into the food processor.

Date paste is a fantastic alternative to sugar in primal baking.

DATE PASTE

Makes 1½ cups

2 cups dried, pitted dates

Place dates in a bowl and pour boiling water over them so they are completely submerged. Allow to sit for 30–40 minutes, then strain the dates, reserving the liquid.

Place dates in a food processor and let it run for a few minutes until dates are completely smooth. You may need to add a bit of the strained date liquid if the mixture stays too chunky.

A mild-flavoured honey is best for this curd, so it does not overpower the flavour of the grapefruit.

GRAPEFRUIT CURD

Makes about 2½ cups

- 125 g butter, at room temperature
- ⅔ cup mild-flavoured honey
- 4 eggs, at room temperature
- ½ cup fresh pink grapefruit juice
- zest of 1 large or 2 small grapefruits

Using a stand mixer or a hand-held beater, cream butter and honey together until smooth and creamy.

While mixing, add eggs one at a time until fully incorporated, scraping down the bowl after each addition. Mix in grapefruit juice and zest.

Pour the curd mixture into a small saucepan over a medium heat. Cook, stirring constantly, until the mixture just begins to thicken – do not allow it to boil.

Once thickened, remove from the heat, pour through a sieve into a clean jar or lidded bowl, and allow it to cool completely. It will continue to thicken as it cools. Store covered in the refrigerator.

My grandmother always had apple butter on the kitchen table for the family to have on English muffins for breakfast. It's traditionally made with loads of sugar, but really doesn't need to be – the fruit is sweet enough on its own.

APPLE–PEAR COMPOTE

Makes about 3 cups

- 1 kg sweet apples (Fuji is good)
- 1 kg ripe pears
- 1 tbsp Vanilla Extract (page 168)
- 2 tbsp lemon juice
- 1½ tbsp ground cinnamon
- 1 tsp allspice
- 2 cups water

Peel and core the fruit and chop into small chunks. Place in a large pot or a slow-cooker.

Stir in vanilla, lemon juice, cinnamon and allspice, then pour water over the top.

Cook, covered, over a low heat for 8–10 hours (pot or slow-cooker), stirring occasionally. The fruit will be nearly mush, and much of the liquid will have evaporated.

Blend cooked fruit and juices in a food processor or with a stick blender. It should be thick and smooth. Store in an airtight container in the refrigerator.

To me, it's gotta be real vanilla extract, not that chemical stuff. Good thing you can make it yourself! Disclaimer – vodka isn't exactly primal, but used in an extract you would eat such a negligible quantity that it shouldn't affect your healthy lifestyle goals.

VANILLA EXTRACT

Makes 500 ml

4–5 vanilla pods
500 ml bottle vodka

Split vanilla pods in half lengthwise and scrape out the seeds. Put the pods and seeds into the vodka bottle, twist the lid on tightly, and give it a shake.

That's it! Store the extract in a cool, dry place. The longer it has to sit, the better and stronger the flavour will be. Just give it a shake once in a while.

Cook's Note

You can use the same process to make other natural flavours. To make almond extract, substitute the vanilla pods for ¼ cup blanched almonds. For lemon or other citrus extracts, mix vodka with fresh citrus peels. Peppermint extract? Combine vodka with fresh peppermint leaves. Try this with any of your favourite flavours!

A great topping for all sorts of desserts!

WHIPPED COCONUT CREAM

Makes 2½ cups

1 can (425 ml) coconut cream
½ tsp Vanilla Extract (above)

Chill coconut cream in refrigerator overnight. The next day, empty the can into a large bowl, add Vanilla Extract and whip with electric beaters, or by hand, until it forms soft peaks.

Most chutneys are completely loaded with sugar, which I find totally unnecessary – especially when you're cooking with a fruit as sweet as pineapple. This is a great accompaniment to my Spicy Cajun Prawns (page 61), but you can use it with any dish you like.

PINEAPPLE CHUTNEY

Makes 2 cups

500 g canned crushed pineapple, including juice (or fresh if you've got it)

1 cup cider vinegar

4 cloves garlic, finely diced

1 tsp chilli flakes (use more or less, depending on how spicy you like it)

1 tsp grated fresh ginger

salt to taste

Combine all ingredients in a saucepan. Bring to a boil then reduce to a low simmer, stirring occasionally, for about 15–20 minutes until the sauce reduces and becomes quite thick.

That's it! Cool and store in an airtight container in the refrigerator.

FIVE DAYS OF PRIMAL:
Fitting healthy eating into your busy week

A common excuse people use for not eating healthily is that they just don't have the time. Another is that they don't know where to begin, so they never begin at all! The best way to keep up with a healthy eating routine is to do a little bit of prep work. Here are some tips to help you get started:

- Spend an hour on Sunday afternoon making a big batch of Famous Cinnamon Vanilla Granola (page 16), or make and freeze a tray of Hearty Savoury Muffins (page 44) to have on hand for breakfast during the week.
- Make and freeze meals ahead of time – you'll be glad you did later. Dishes like meatloaf, curry and puréed soups are simple to make and freeze well.
- Make good use of a slow-cooker, and let it do all the work for you. Throw your ingredients in before work and by the time you get home, dinner is ready!
- Don't be afraid of eating non-breakfast foods for breakfast. You can eat eggs for dinner, so why not have steak for breakfast?
- Do your best to balance protein, fats and carbs within your day's meals. Honey and dates are primal ingredients, but if you eat heaps of the sweet stuff and nothing else, you are not likely to get the full benefits of a primal diet.

Here's what a week of eating primal looks like in my kitchen:

MONDAY

Breakfast – ½ cup Cocoa Hazelnut Granola (page 19) with a dollop of Greek yoghurt and fresh (or frozen) berries

Lunch – Chicken and Pumpkin Curry with Mango Chutney (page 77) prepared the night before.

Dinner – 'Breaded' Chicken (page 78) with Golden Kumara Mash (page 148) and a green salad

TUESDAY

Breakfast – The Lazy Cook's Breakfast Scramble (page 31)

Lunch – Kitchen Sink Salad (page 57) using leftover chicken from Monday night's dinner

Dinner – Meaty Stuffed Capsicums (page 89)

Dessert – Baked Nutty Apple Crumble (page 133) with fresh whipped cream

WEDNESDAY

Breakfast – Super-powered Breakfast Smoothie (page 23)

Lunch – German-style Sausages with Roasted Cabbage, Apple and Caraway (page 86)

Dinner – Red Wine Braised Short Ribs with Sautéed Mushrooms and Leek (page 90)

THURSDAY

Breakfast – Baked Egg and Veggie Hash (page 32) with leftover veggies from Wednesday night's dinner

Lunch – Butternut Squash and Sage Soup (page 50), thawed from the giant batch I stash in the freezer

Snack – one or two Energy Bites (page 20)

Dinner – Lemon, Garlic and Thyme Roasted Chicken and Root Veggies (page 70)

Dessert – Baked Sweet Kumara Custard (page 118)

FRIDAY

Breakfast – Banana Streusel Muffin (page 43)

Lunch – Kitchen Sink Salad (page 57) with chicken from Thursday night's dinner

Dinner – Baked Tarakihi with Lemon and Olives (page 66)

Acknowledgements

I owe so many thanks to everyone who has helped me and inspired me to write this book. I can't possibly fit them all on one page, but I cannot do without thanking the following people.

Agnes, for pushing me to get this book published, and for all the times I invaded your kitchen for an ingredient, some advice, or just a cup of tea and a yarn. I adore you.

Kieran, for teaching me how to eat fat. Seriously.

The Hania Street crew, for being my first customers, and for giving me the confidence to take all of this (literally) outside the box.

Most importantly, my parents, for your unconditional love and support my whole life, even when I told you I was going to move to the other side of the world.

I love you all and couldn't have done this without you!

A huge thank you to Moore Wilson's, Vessel and Heritage Tiles for their support and for lending us the beautiful props used in this book, and to Ceres Fresh Market and Ponsonby Central for allowing us to use their space for photography.

Index